Evaluation of Agricultural Policy Reforms in the European Union

THE COMMON AGRICULTURAL POLICY 2014-20

This work is published under the responsibility of the Secretary-General of the OECD. The opinions expressed and arguments employed herein do not necessarily reflect the official views of OECD member countries.

This document and any map included herein are without prejudice to the status of or sovereignty over any territory, to the delimitation of international frontiers and boundaries and to the name of any territory, city or area.

Please cite this publication as:
OECD (2017), *Evaluation of Agricultural Policy Reforms in the European Union: The Common Agricultural Policy 2014-20*, OECD Publishing, Paris.
http://dx.doi.org/10.1787/9789264278783-en

ISBN 978-92-64-27868-4 (print)
ISBN 978-92-64-27878-3 (PDF)

The statistical data for Israel are supplied by and under the responsibility of the relevant Israeli authorities. The use of such data by the OECD is without prejudice to the status of the Golan Heights, East Jerusalem and Israeli settlements in the West Bank under the terms of international law.

Photo credits: Cover © Michal Kaco/Shutterstock.com.

Corrigenda to OECD publications may be found on line at: *www.oecd.org/about/publishing/corrigenda.htm.*
© OECD 2017

Foreword

Successive reforms have shaped the European Union's agricultural policy. This report offers an evaluation of the main new features of the Common Agricultural Policy (CAP) over the 2014-20 period. It notes that in many ways the CAP 2014-20 is a continuation of the previous CAP while also offering some novel features. Starting with the description of the new institutional context whereby it was co-signed by Council and Parliament, the report then reviews the new policy features. New compulsory measures are introduced within an overall stable budget. These include the greening payment that is conditional on farming practices deemed to deliver specific environmental outcomes, and also the payment to support newly installed young farmers. The CAP 2014-20 also allows for greater flexibility. Member states may now partly tailor the implementation of some compulsory measures to their own conditions, they may also adopt choice measures from a menu of direct payments. Member states have embraced to varying degrees these new opportunities for flexibility. Their choices are discussed in this report. The OECD Producer Support Estimate (PSE) framework that quantifies policy transfers and the CAPRI model of European agriculture are used to offer an *ex ante* assessment of public expenditure associated with the new measures.Two policy dimensions are discussed in greater detail, first the provision of risk management instruments and their take up by member states and, second, the menu of environmental measures.

Based on these elements, the report draws a number of conclusions and recommendations.

This report offers a timely analysis of the new features of the European Union's main agricultural policy instrument. The review belongs to the longstanding series of Evaluations of Agricultural Policy Reforms and adds to the previous work on the Common Agricultural Policy published in 2011.

Acknowledgements

The main authors of the report are Morvarid Bagherzadeh (project leader), Jo Cadilhon and Václav Vojtech. Research and statistical assistance was provided by Eline Kamgang, Tarja Mard, Karine Souvanheuane, Noura Takrouri Jolly, and Lihan Wei. The CAPRI analysis was carried out by Torbjörn Jansson (Swedish University of Agricultural Sciences), Peter Witzke (EuroCARE Bonn GmbH) and Alexander Gocht (Thünen Institute). Administrative and editorial assistance was provided by Martina Abderrahmane.

The report benefited from the valuable contributions from OECD colleagues and the Working Party on Agricultural Policies and Markets. It was declassified by the Working Party in March 2017.

Table of contents

Figures

Executive summary

This report focuses on the main new features of the CAP 2014-20. It starts by placing the CAP in its institutional context; Chapter 2 offers a description of the main new features of the CAP 2014-20. In Chapter 3, risk management instruments are discussed and assessed. Chapter 4 discusses the environmental measures of the CAP. Based on these elements, the report draws a number of conclusions which are summarised below.

From an institutional point of view

In the new institutional environment defined by the Treaty of Lisbon, the CAP 2014-20 was adopted by co-decision of the European Parliament and Council. The Common Strategic Framework was established. It sets strategic guiding principles for the programming process of sectoral and territorial coordination of European Structural and Investment funds, in line with the Europe 2020 strategy. The conclusion of the Multiannual Financial Framework also influenced the final phases of the agreement on the CAP.

- Adaptation to the co-decision rule was successful and the CAP 2014-20 was approved by all parties in December 2013. However, co-decision led to some lags.

- The new adoption process and the subsequent implementation steps, in particular those related to the approval of rural development programmes took a toll on timing that should be anticipated in future exercises to deliver the next CAP to the farm sector and rural areas without disruption.

- The new monitoring and assessment of measures against policy objectives is a positive development, in particular if intermediate mechanisms are available to adjust policies to better align with objectives, when necessary.

- The monitoring framework could be a powerful driver to overcome lack of data and other statistical limitations.

New features of the CAP 2014-20

In many ways the CAP 2014-20 is a continuation of the CAP 2007-13 and at the same time it offers some novel features. It can be characterised as flexible-binding. While it offers member states many opportunities for flexibility, at the same time, required internal and external convergence largely determine rates of payments per hectare and prescriptive farming conditions apply to the greening payments.

The analysis of the effects on production, prices, trade, welfare and the environment shows that the impact of the policy changes in CAP 2014-20 is likely to be small at the aggregated level. Nonetheless, the results highlight that some redistribution occurs between sectors and between member states, resulting from the combination of a reduced budget for direct payments (basic payment scheme), a larger share of support that is coupled to production and the convergence of per hectare payment rates both within member states (internal) and between member states (external). Results also show that greening is likely to have small aggregate impacts except on some specific land allocations. The analysis also reveals inconsistent signals between measures that encourage production, through commodity coupled support, and the greening payment or other measures that aim to reduce the negative environmental impacts of agriculture. Farm level and social impacts, such as rural development are not measured.

Member states have embraced to varying degrees the increased flexibility in implementation to:

- Move funds towards priority measures by using the possibility to transfer funds between pillars.

- Tailor implementation of compulsory measures to their own specific situations within the limits of the regulations ceilings and thresholds.

- Choose from a wider menu of measures.

As a result of member states' choices, the budgets allocated to compulsory measures have generally decreased and a larger budget is devoted to choice measures, reducing the commonality of the European Union's Agricultural Policy.

- This can be a positive development if measures are targeted to the production of commonly defined outcomes, and their implementation adapted to local conditions.

- The CAP could better target support to remunerate the provision of public goods, such as environmental stewardship and climate change mitigation. Support could be used to facilitate the transition to farming methods that are more resilient to climate risk.

- Public expenditure to support education and research services, to contribute to innovation and encourage its take-up, should be enhanced as these are fundamental to future productivity gains and increased sector resilience.

- Some member states have directed a significant share of the Voluntary Coupled Support to the ruminant livestock sectors. Other, less market and resource distorting means should be considered to support farm holdings' efforts to achieve long-term competitiveness and productivity gains. Short-term income problems should be addressed with risk management tools.

Risk management

Risk management instruments of the CAP have received limited take up by member states. They include insurance premium subsidies and support to mutual funds. However, many more measures and payments directly or indirectly influence the risk exposure of farmers and should hence be included in a holistic assessment of risk management instruments. Although risk management measures under the second pillar receive limited take up, monitoring and evaluating member states' implementation choices would allow information sharing and would be a first step towards assessing the need for adaptations.

- The design of effective risk management policies requires that the activation conditions for exceptional public assistance are defined in advance and farmers informed of the conditions as well as the modalities by which such assistance is delivered before risks materialise.

- Effective risk management policies in EU agricultural policy require an integrated approach that addresses all risk exposure and incentives, distinguishes between normal, marketable and catastrophic risk and articulates the respective roles of public authorities and economic actors, including them in the development of risk management strategies based on sound economic analysis of the three risk layers.

- Policies influencing risk exposure and incentives must be considered "holistically." Many policies in the CAP have some impact on risk exposure. A large share of public expenditure support is delivered through payments which guarantee farmers a minimum income. One-fifth of farm receipts result from policies that cushion the impacts of downward income fluctuations. This may lower the incentives to take up the specific risk management measures on offer or to develop private risk management approaches.

- Institutional frameworks for private insurance and financial institutions should be present to offer the necessary services.

- Co-responsibility of farmers should be maintained and enhanced. Incentives to take up measures that imply co-funding and co-responsibility are low as long as farmers can assume that public assistance will be forthcoming in case of "exceptional circumstances".

- Collecting evidence on farm household income and enhancing information systems would be necessary for any well-functioning income insurance system.

Environmental components

Through time the CAP has developed a range of policy measures that address the environmental impacts of agriculture. Since 2005, cross-compliance is compulsory and applies to most direct payments. It consists of statutory management requirements, in other words complying with legislative standards, and standards for Good Agricultural and Environmental Conditions. The CAP 2014-20 introduces a new greening payment that makes 30% of the direct payments budget conditional on adhering to specific farming practices that come in addition to the existing cross-compliance. The expenditure budgets numbers show that a higher share has been used. The analysis shows that the conditions specified to qualify for the greening payment require a change in farming practices in only a few areas, compared to existing cross-compliance. The Ecological Focus Area (EFA) condition under greening is expected to have a positive impact on land use. The net effects of the measure on the environment cannot be evaluated at this stage.

In the CAP 2014-20, the denomination of pillar 2 agri-environmental measures has been broadened to include climate. Member states have the flexibility to adapt pillar 2 measures, including agri-environment and climate measures to local conditions. Member states also have flexibility on budgets attributed to pillar 2 measures. As such these measures, that can be scaled financially and targeted locally, have the potential to be better adapted to local conditions than the broad based and uniform greening payment.

- Over the long-term, the share of producer support subject to mandatory constraints (cross-compliance) or compensating for the additional costs of voluntary environmental constraints has grown. The trend indicates the growing importance of environmental objectives within the European Union's agricultural agenda.

- However, domestic programmes concomitantly apply in member states; most of which are not subject to cross-compliance or other environmental constraints.

- The principles of greening require that all farms are subjected to the same conditions to receive support. The approach has the advantage of common and broad coverage. However, since the agri-environmental circumstances are very heterogeneous across member states and farms, a complex system of "equivalences" was developed. The effectiveness of this solution remains to be seen. An alternative design would directly target environmental outcomes at the farm level, as opposed to encouraging certain practices that are deemed to be environmentally beneficial. The difficulty of measuring environmental outcomes at farm level should not be underestimated, and improved access to technology may offer viable solutions in the future.

- Environmental effects of greening measures will depend on the specific implementation in each member state. The positive effects of greening conditions would be enhanced by monitoring the correct implementation of greening requirements and providing advisory services to farmers to adapt choices to the local environmental conditions. Most EU farmers have already met the crop diversification requirement. The obligation to manage 5% of agricultural land as EFA is expected to have a positive effect and increase land set-aside. This could, in turn, increase intensive practices (within permitted limits) on remaining productive land. The overall impact of greening on EU aggregate production, prices and trade is likely to be marginal, local effects could be more notable.

- The new Agri-environment and climate measures are a direct continuation of the former agri-environmental payments; more assessments will be needed to evaluate their additional impact. They are likely to yield environmental benefits at the local level as they improve the targeting and local relevance of member states expenditure. Furthermore, member states may choose to decentralise their implementation to a regional level, thus increasing the potential for better targeting support to local objectives and conditions.

- Agri-environmental policies use a voluntary approach to enhance the environmental performance of the farming sector. However, through its pillar 1 support measures the CAP also provides incentives to produce. These may, in turn, increase pressure on natural resources. Policy coherence would require a comprehensive review of all measures affecting environmental performance of the farming sector in the European Union together with an assessment of local environmental conditions.

Chapter 1

A new institutional context

The Treaty of Lisbon defined a new institutional environment whereby, for the first time, the Common Agricultural Policy for 2014-20 was adopted by co-decision between the European Parliament and the Council. Co-decision was also the rule for adopting the European Union's multiannual financial framework (MFF). The MFF sets ceilings for EU spending for the seven-year period between 2014 and 2020 and defines the financial boundaries of the Common Agricultural Policy. Monitoring and evaluation are strengthened in the CAP 2014-20 and tools are foreseen to assess the outcome of the CAP against the European Union's policy objectives. Results are reported to the European Parliament and to the Council. These new institutional features of the CAP are described in this chapter.

The European Union's Common Agricultural Policy (CAP) is the main agricultural policy instrument of the European Union. But the CAP is not only about agriculture and, while 96% of the CAP budget supports agriculture, it also covers forestry and some more general services destined to rural areas with the remaining funds. European Union member states may also implement domestic policies that support agriculture, in addition to the CAP. The focus of this report is confined to the CAP and agriculture; more specifically the expected effects of new measures of the CAP 2014-20 on the agricultural sector. Farm level and social impacts, such as rural development are not measured.

The adoption of the CAP 2014-20 was carried out in a new institutional environment defined by the Treaty of Lisbon. Most importantly, it meant that for the first time the CAP was adopted by co-decision between the European Parliament and the Council[1] (Box 1.1). While the process formulating the new policies started in 2010, 2014 was a transition year with the introduction of pillar 1; implemented in full in 2015, while the full implementation by member states of pillar 2 measures occurred in 2016. This has meant that the transition between the CAP 2007-13 and the CAP 2014-20 resulted in delayed spending.

Co-decision was also the rule for adopting the European Union's multiannual financial framework (MFF) that sets ceilings for EU spending for the seven-year period between 2014 and 2020 (Box 1.2). In 2016 some adjustments were proposed which have not been agreed to this date: an increase of EUR 1.8 billion for the year 2017 (EU Budget, 2016); a mid-term review of the MFF by which an additional EUR 6.3 billion would be funded over 2017-20 for jobs and growth, migration and security (EC, 2016b); and the creation of a new instrument, the EU Crisis reserve, that would be provisioned for in the EU budget; using de-committed appropriations from previous budget years, in order to keep within the overall ceiling agreed under the MFF. The MFF has proven its value in keeping expenses mostly under check while also being responsive to situation changes. However, the lack of evaluative indicators that would assess impact against policy objectives and targets makes adjustments harder to explain.

Box 1.1. Co-decision and the CAP 2014-20

With the entry into force of the Treaty of Lisbon of December 2009, co-decision became the general rule for adopting legislation at European Union level. The European Parliament (EP) and the Council were engaged jointly to adopt the CAP 2014-20 based on the publication in November 2010 of the European Commission's Communication (EC, 2010) and the legislative proposals in October 2011 on the four CAP regulations: Direct Payments, Rural Development, Common Market Organisation and the Horizontal Regulation.

The legislative proposals were presented to the EP and the Council, the co-legislators of the texts, for a processing phase which took place from October 2011 to April 2013 (EP, 2014a).[1] Meanwhile, a parallel process was underway for the adoption of the multiannual financial framework (MFF) and in February 2013 an agreement was reached on the ceilings of EU spending from 2014 till 2020 (OJ, 2013a).

The adoption process of the CAP involved informal negotiations between representatives of the Council, the Parliament and the Commission, so-called trilogues. Trilogues were used to reconcile positions and clear the way for the adoption of the act. The negotiating phase took place between April 2013 and June 2013 and about 50 trilogues were needed before a political agreement was reached on 26 June 2013 on the basic acts of the four regulations. The EP approved the four Basic Regulations in a plenary vote on 20 November 2013 and on 16 December 2013 the Council formally adopted the four Basic Regulations for the CAP 2014-20 as well as the Transition Rules for 2014. These were published on 20 December 2013 in the Official Journal of the European Union (OJ, 2013b, 2013c, 2013d and 2013e).

Delegated acts clarifying the implementation details of the CAP 2014-20 were adopted by the Commission on 11 March 2014 and approved by the EP and Council in April 2014.

Member states could then in turn decide choice elements of the Direct Payments and develop their Partnership Agreements outlining their strategic objectives that would define their Rural Development Programmes (RDP), for submission to and approval by the European Commission (EC, 2016a). Member states submitted 118 RDP and the approval process was completed in December 2015 and the full scope of payments related to the CAP 2014-20 could be disbursed subsequently, (ENRD, 2015).

---

1. Details and analysis of the process can be found in the European Parliament report *The first CAP reform under the ordinary legislative procedure: a political economy perspective* (EP, 2014a)

Box 1.2. The European Union's Multiannual financial framework

The multiannual financial framework (MFF) lays down the maximum amounts, ceilings, which the European Union may spend. The current MFF organises EU spending across six headings and extends over the 2014-20 period. The framework defines a) an annual ceiling for each heading, these are legally binding promises to spend money which, if not spent in the year, may be disbursed over several financial years; b) an overall annual ceiling corresponding to the sum of each heading ceilings; and c) an overall annual ceiling actual amounts authorized for disbursement in a given year.

Considering the distribution across headings, as shown in Figure 1.1, the second heading; Sustainable growth: natural resources of which the CAP is the main component could take up nearly 40% of the overall ceiling.

Figure 1.1. Multiannual Financial Framework 2014-20

Overall ceiling of EUR 1 087 billion (2016 prices)

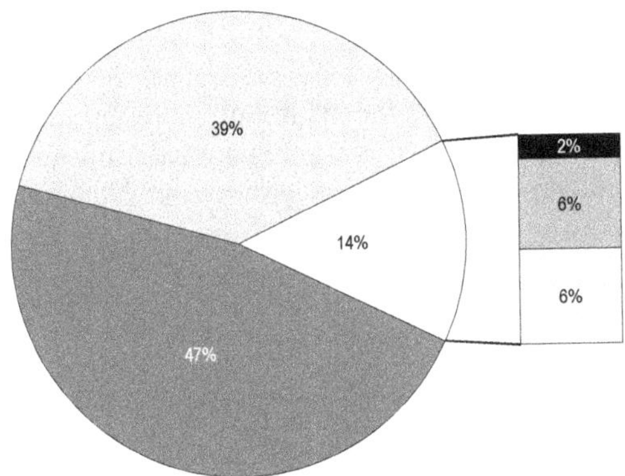

Source: European Commission, Figures and documents of the multiannual financial framework webpage, http://ec.europa.eu/budget/mff/figures/index_en.cfm (accessed on 25 October 2016).

While the MFF aims to enforce budgetary discipline on EU spending, it allows for flexibility through a number of mechanisms and instruments. A total budget of EUR 1.4 billion is set aside annually under four funds to allow for intervention in non-EU countries (Emergency Aid Reserve of EUR 0.2 billion), disaster mitigation (Solidarity Fund of EUR 0.5 billion), unplanned expenditure (Flexibility instrument of EUR 0.5 billion) and re-employment (European Globalisation Adjustment Fund with EUR 0.2 billion). Unspent monies under these funds can be carried over to the next year and special provisions are made to bring forward monies to support Youth employment.

Another new institutional feature is the inclusion of better monitoring and evaluation in the policy cycle. Annex 1.A1 gives a detailed description of the implementation of the monitoring and evaluation process. The provisions in the CAP 2007-13 to monitor its implementation (OJ, 2005), were mostly to control and to contain financial risks. A new common monitoring and evaluation framework of the measures is now part of the CAP 2014-20 whereby:

> *Each measure under the CAP should be subject to monitoring and evaluation in order to improve its quality and to demonstrate its achievements.* (OJ, 2013b).

The European Commission is tasked to draw up a list of performance indicators to assess the outcome of the measures against three policy objectives: viable food production, the sustainable management of natural resources and climate action and balanced territorial development. A new "Common Monitoring and Evaluation Framework" (CMEF) has been set up. The framework entails the availability and timeliness of relevant data. The key tool employed in the CMEF is a set of indicators that can be classified in four types: a) context indicators; b) output indicators; c) result indicators; and d) impact indicators. A first publication of the full set of indicators is planned in 2017. The task is formidable considering the diversity of the Union's statistical landscape and the lack of comparable data on some of the prominent objectives of the CAP, including sustainability (Koester and Loy, 2016). The statistical framework should not only address current needs but also anticipate the future and collect and publish data needed to assess measures supporting productivity gains and innovation.

In addition to monitoring indicators, the CMEF also commissions evaluation studies from external experts. A first such study analysed member states implementation choices for the CAP 2014-20. This comprehensive analysis of member state choices notes the new flexibilities under pillar 1, the changes of the structure of pillar 2, as well as the improved coordination between pillars. The CAP is more complex and its implementation, management and reporting has become more burdensome for central and local authorities. Farmers may see an increase in the amount of evidence they have to provide (EC, 2016c).

The Common Strategic Framework sets strategic guiding principles for the programming process of sectoral and territorial coordination of Union intervention under the European Structural and Investment (ESI) funds, including the European Agricultural Fund for Rural Development, in line with the targets and objectives of the Europe 2020 strategy.

Note

1.   The Council of the European Union is the institution representing the member states' governments. Also known informally as the EU Council, it is where national ministers from each EU country meet to adopt laws and co-ordinate policies. The European Union counts 28 member states.

References

EC (2016a), "Rural development 2014-20", European Commission, Brussels, http://ec.europa.eu/agriculture/rural-development-2014-2020/index_en.htm, (accessed on 25 October 2016).

EC (2016b), Communication from the Commission to the European Parliament and the Council, "Mid-term review/revision of the multiannual financial framework 2014-2020", European Commission, Brussels, http://ec.europa.eu/budget/mff/lib/COM-2016-603/COM-2016-603_en.pdf.

EC (2016c), "Mapping and analysis of the implementation of the CAP", Directorate-General for Agriculture and Rural Development, European Commission, Brussels, https://ec.europa.eu/agriculture/sites/agriculture/files/external-studies/2016/mapping-analysis-implementation-cap/fullrep_en.pdf

EC (2010), Communication from the Commission to the European Parliament, the Council, the European Economic and Social Committee and the Committee of the Regions: "The CAP towards 2020: Meeting the food, natural resources and territorial challenges of the future", European Commission, Brussels, http://eur-lex.europa.eu/legal-content/EN/TXT/PDF/?uri=CELEX:52010DC0672&rid=5.

ENRD (2015), "RDP planning, European network for rural development", European Commission, Brussels, https://enrd.ec.europa.eu/policy-in-action/cap-towards-2020/rdp-programming-2014-2020/rdp-planning_en (accessed on 25 October 2016).

EP (2014a), "Decision and Conciliation, A guide to how the European Parliament co-legislates under the ordinary legislative procedure", European Parliament, Brussels.

EP (2014b), "The first CAP reform under the ordinary legislative procedure: a political economy perspective", European Parliament, Brussels.

EU Budget (2016), Letter of amendment No. 1/2017, European Union, http://eur-lex.europa.eu/budget/www/index-en.htm.

Koester, U. and JP. Loy (2016), "EU Agricultural Policy Reform: Evaluating the EU's New Methodology for Direct Payments", *Intereconomics* (2016) 51: 278.

Official Journal of the European Union (OJ) (2013a), Council Regulation No 1311/2013 laying down the multiannual financial framework for the years 2014-2020, Brussels.

OJ (2013b), Regulation (EU) No 1306/2013 of the European Parliament and of the Council on the financing, management and monitoring of the common agricultural policy, Brussels.

OJ (2013c), Regulation (EU) No 1305/2013 of the European Parliament and of the Council on support for rural development by the European Agricultural Fund for Rural Development (EAFRD), Brussels.

OJ (2013d), Regulation (EU) No 1307/2013 of the European Parliament and of the Council establishing rules for direct payments to farmers under support schemes within the framework of the common agricultural policy, Brussels.

OJ (2013e), Regulation (EU) No 1308/2013 of the European Parliament and of the Council establishing a common organisation of the markets in agricultural products, Brussels.

OJ (2005), Council Regulation No 1290/2005 on the financing of the common agricultural policy, Brussels.

Annex 1.A1

Common monitoring and evaluation framework[1]

Origin

As part of the CAP (2014-20) and in accordance with Article 110 of Regulation (EU) No 1306/2013, for the first time, a "Common Monitoring and Evaluation Framework" (CMEF) has been set up to measure the performance of the whole CAP (both pillar 1 direct payments to farmers and market measures and pillar 2 rural development measures).

Additionally, a Common Monitoring and Evaluation System (CMES), which is part of the CMEF, was established by Regulations (EU) No 1303/2013, for the European Structural and Investment Funds (ESIF) and Regulation (EU) No 1305/2013, for the specificities in the rural development programmes.

CMEF Expert Group

The CMEF is overseen by the Expert Group on Monitoring and Evaluating the CAP (Expert Group), which provides a forum for evaluation experts from all the member states and the European Commission to exchange experiences, examples of good practices and information on all evaluation-related issues. Specific pillar 2 issues are discussed with a focus on technical aspects and with the aim of providing guidance and support to member states concerning the organisation and implementation of their rural development evaluations. Pillar 1 evaluations, which are under the responsibility of the European Commission, are also presented within this group.

Aim of the CMEF

In the EU lexicon, monitoring is considered to be "the continuous task of reviewing information and systematic stocktaking of budgetary inputs and financed activities". Its main aim is to demonstrate the progress on the implementation of the policy

Evaluation is the "judgement of interventions according to the results, impacts and the needs they aim to satisfy," according to criteria of effectiveness, relevance, coherence and EU added value. Evaluation is carried out to provide useful and timely conclusions and policy recommendations.

Together, monitoring and evaluation provide an analytical basis for future policy design by giving a better understanding of the effectiveness of measures and the achievement of set objectives; helping in setting policy and programme objectives, especially over the long-term; and contributing to the accountability of public spending.

Performance against objectives

In the CMEF, the performance of CAP measures is assessed in relation to the three general objectives of the CAP (i.e. viable food production; sustainable management of natural resources and climate action; and balanced territorial development) and, in the case of pillar 2, in relation to the thematic objectives for the Europe 2020 strategy for smart, sustainable and inclusive growth. Within the general CAP objectives, there are a number of specific CAP objectives as reflected in Figure 1.A1.1.

Figure 1.A1.1. CAP objectives and intervention instruments

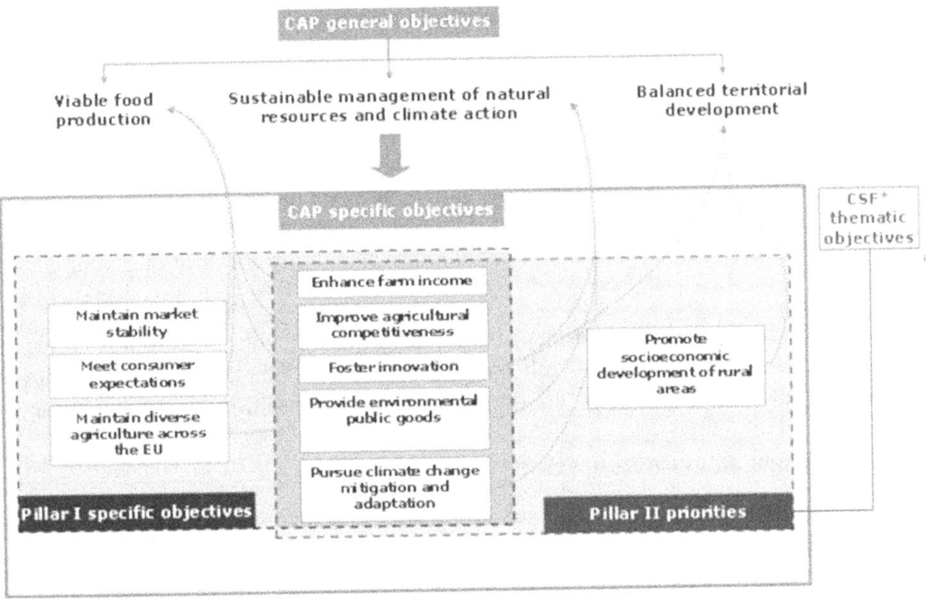

Source: European Commission.

Indicators

The key tool employed in the CMEF is a set of indicators, which measure the degree of achievement of an objective, in terms of resources mobilised, an output accomplished or an effect obtained, or to describe the context (economic, social or environmental).

Four types of indicator, listed in Regulation (EC) No 834/2014,[2] were established:

- Forty-five context indicators, which measure general background trends in the economy, the agricultural sector and environment.

- A total of 84 output indicators, which measure activities directly realised by the policy interventions in the areas of direct payments (36), markets (13), horizontal aspects (9, in areas such as cross-compliance, quality, organic farming, promotion, farm advisory system) and rural development (26).

- A total of 65 result indicators, for both pillar 1 (16) result indicators and pillar 2 (25), as well as 24 target indicators for rural development, which measure direct and immediate effects of interventions.

- Sixteen impact indicators for general CAP objectives, which measure outcomes of policy interventions, beyond immediate effects.

Since the CAP is implemented through shared management, the information used for compiling these indicators is largely obtained from member states. When designing the monitoring and evaluation framework, particular attention was paid to the issues of proportionality, simplification and a reduction of the administrative burden. As a result, the total number of indicators has been limited, and emphasis has been put on the use of indicators based, to the extent possible, on existing, well-established data sources, as well as reuse of information already provided by member states. The use of these well-established data sources also contributes to the reliability of the indicators.

For each of the indicators used, a detailed information sheet has been produced explaining the exact data definition, data source, level of geographical detail, reporting frequency and delay, etc., to make sure that all data providers work on the same basis and that data users understand what the data represent. Furthermore, during this process of building the indicator dataset, the feasibility, usefulness and coverage provided by the chosen indicators is constantly being assessed and, should any adjustments be necessary, they will be made in due course.

Evaluation studies

While monitoring is largely a direct responsibility of public authorities, evaluations of pillar 1 measures are carried out by independent external contractors, under the responsibility of the Commission services, on the basis of a multiannual evaluation plan.[3] The independent external contractor carries out the evaluation according to the terms of references under the supervision of a steering group in a given, contractually fixed time period.

For pillar 2, on the other hand, evaluations of the rural development programmes are carried out by, or on behalf of, the member states while the synthesis of these evaluations at EU level, and evaluation of the joint effects of pillar 1 and pillar 2 measures, are done under the responsibility of the European Commission.

Publication of monitoring and evaluation results

Evaluation results are made publicly available, for the time being separately for market and income measures,[4] and for rural development policy.[5] These reports are also communicated to all relevant decision-makers (e.g. the European Parliament, the Council and the European Court of Auditors) and other interested stakeholders.

Regarding the monitoring results, public access to all information is being rolled out in 2017. The European Commission already provides an annual update of data (subject to availability) of the CAP context indicators, and their explanatory fiches.[6]

Information, including evaluation reports, on EU rural development policy and individual member state rural development programmes is provided on a dedicated webpage,[7] which also gives a link to the Open Portal of the ESIF,[8] allowing access to the distribution of finances and (selected) planned achievements under the six different funds according to the 11 common themes.

It is planned to have the full set of indicators of the CMEF, with their detailed information sheets, available to the public during the course of 2017.

Reporting obligations on the implementation of the CAP

There are obligations attached to the monitoring and evaluation effort in the CMEF. In accordance with Article 318 of the Treaty on the Functioning of the European Union, the Commission must report to the European Parliament and to the Council. The first report, due in 2018, will focus on policy implementation and first results. A more complete assessment of the impact of the CAP is expected by 2021.

Specifically for pillar 2, EC Implementing Regulation 808/2014 on support for rural development foresees that member states submit each year, since 2016 and until 2024, an annual implementation report (AIR) on the RDP implementation of the previous calendar year. The regulation has made provision for an enhanced AIR to be submitted in 2017 and 2019 that covers additional information resulting from evaluation activities. These reports cover the implementation of the partnership agreement,[9] set at member state level on all ESI funds in order to ensure alignment with the Europe 2020 strategy, as well as the fund-specific objectives.

Notes to Annex 1.A1

1. The description of the Common monitoring and evaluation framework (CMEF) was prepared by the European Commission. The CMEF is a process established by EU Regulations. It is not related to OECD evaluations of agricultural policies. While the two processes may inform one another, they are conducted independently.

2. http://eur-lex.europa.eu/legal-content/EN/TXT/PDF/?uri=CELEX:32014R0834&from=EN.

3. http://ec.europa.eu/agriculture/sites/agriculture/files/evaluation/plan_en.pdf.

4. https://ec.europa.eu/agriculture/evaluation/market-and-income-reports_en.

5. https://ec.europa.eu/agriculture/evaluation/rural-development-reports_en.

6. https://ec.europa.eu/agriculture/cap-indicators/context_en.

7. https://ec.europa.eu/agriculture/rural-development-2014-2020_en.

8. https://cohesiondata.ec.europa.eu/funds/eafrd.

9. A "Partnership agreement" is a member state's strategy, priorities and arrangements for using the ESI Funds, which is approved by the Commission following assessment and dialogue with the member state concerned.

Chapter 2

Main components of the CAP

> *In many ways the CAP 2014-20 can be characterised as a continuation of the CAP 2007-13. Its overall funding is almost constant and the two-pillar structure is maintained. At the same time, new measures, increased flexibility and more binding instruments are introduced. This chapter points to those features that are continued from the previous CAP and discusses the new developments. Member states' implementation choices are described and associated public expenditure are detailed. The OECD PSE framework that quantifies policy transfers and the CAPRI model of European agriculture are used to offer an ex ante assessment of the new measures.*

2.1. The CAP 2014-20 and its funding

In many ways the CAP 2014-20 can be characterised as a continuation of the CAP 2007-13 (OECD, 2011). The overall funding is almost constant and the two-pillar structure is maintained. At the same time new measures, increased flexibility and more binding instruments are introduced that may serve to test future CAP reform. This chapter describes the main components of the CAP 2014-20; it points to those features that are continued and discusses the new developments.

The CAP 2014-20 was formally adopted in December 2013. It was implemented progressively starting in 2014 (Box 1.1 in Chapter 1). Concurrently member states developed and put forward their national Rural Development Programmes (RDP) under pillar 2 (Box 2.2). Overall, 118 national and regional RDP were developed by member states and their approval by the Commission was completed in December 2015. Related payments from pillar 2 could be disbursed subsequently and 2016 is the first year where all payments foreseen in the CAP 2014-20 materialise. Market measures and most of the direct payments are funded by the European Agricultural Guarantee Fund (EAGF), also called pillar 1. Measures based on Rural Development Programmes put forward by EU member states are funded from the European Agricultural Fund for Rural Development (EAFRD) also called pillar 2 and co-financed by member states (Table 2.1). The co-financing rate is determined by EU regulation and the EU contribution is higher in less developed regions.

Table 2.1. Overall CAP budget by funding source EU28 over the full 2014-20 cycle

EUR billion current prices and share in Total

	Common Market Organisation (Pillar 1) EU funding	Direct Payments (Pillar 1) EU funding	Rural Development (Pillar 2) EU funding	Rural Development (Pillar 2) member states co-financing and top-ups	Total including CMO
CAP budget EU funding	17	250	100		367
% of Total	5%	68%	27%		100%
CAP budget including co-financing and top-ups	17	250	100	59	426
% of Total	4%	59%	23%	14%	100%

Note: Budgets represented are after transfers between pillars and may be subject to revisions as from budget year 2018.

Source: CAP 2014-20 Budget after transfers between pillars, as published and OECD calculations based on national 2014-20 RDP budget as published in: http://ec.europa.eu/agriculture/rural-development-2014-2020/country-files/index_en.htm, 2016.

The overall budget of the CAP, including co-funding and top-ups by member states, adds up to EUR 426 billion over the seven years of the CAP 2014-20 lifespan, of which 14% is funded by member states. Statutory co-funding ratios vary according to the type of payments and regions. When taking into account the additional amounts of top-ups, the shares of member states' funding of the CAP from own budgets vary from about 50% in Finland and Luxembourg to less than 5% in Denmark, Croatia and Slovenia (Figure 2.1). The common market organisation (CMO) measures represent 4% of the overall budget and are spent at EU level, except for wine, cotton and olive oil that are attributed to member states. The remaining 96%, including the EAGF (pillar 1) direct payments and EAFRD (pillar 2) rural development budgets, are attributed to member states, who in turn allocate them according to policy choices (Figure 2.1).

Taking into consideration pillar 1 direct payments to farmers, and those expenditures on rural development programmes that are implemented as direct transfers to farms, the share of the CAP agricultural expenditure transferred to farms is 90% (Figure 2.3). Figure 2.2 shows the total amount of public spending as a ratio of the value of agricultural goods output in order to correct differences in the economic size of the sector. The calculations assume that public spending is evenly disbursed across the 2014-20 period. An average annual spending is calculated that is then related to the value of agricultural goods output in 2016. Because the output value does not take into account budgetary expenditures, the calculation results do not represent the share of public spending in farm receipts. In the European Union, on average, public spending compares with 16% of the output value of the sector. The numbers compare the size of public spending to the value of output of the sector. In this respect, it is interesting to compare Figure 2.2 results with Figure 2.1. As an example and to illustrate this, Finland accounts for about 3% of CAP public spending of which it contributes more than half from the national budget through statutory co-financing and top-ups (Figure 2.1). In Finland, total public spending compares to about half the size of agricultural output in 2016 (Figure 2.2). In the Netherlands, Belgium and Denmark public receipts compare to less than 10% of agricultural output. These member states receive small shares of total CAP spending while they source respectively 15%, 20% and 6% of the funds from national budgets.

Figure 2.1. Member states CAP budget by funding source for 2014-20 and share in EU28 (excluding CMO)

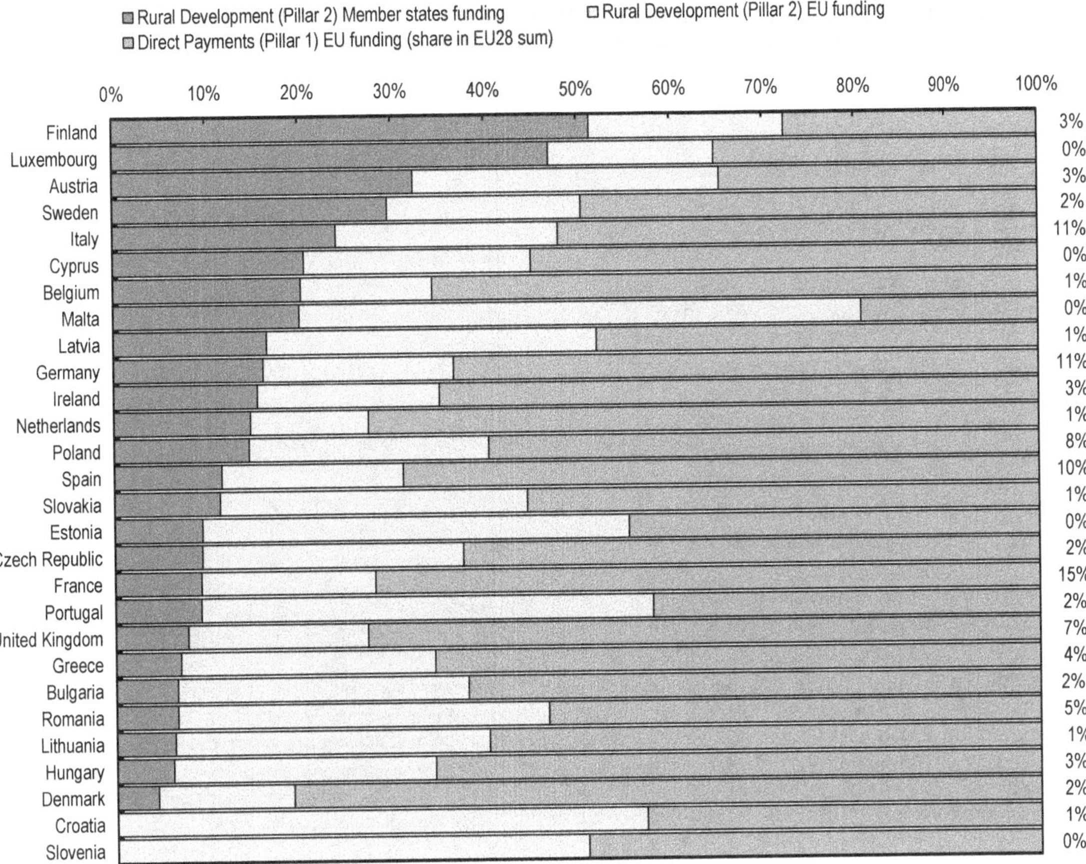

Note: Budgets represented are after transfers between pillars and may be subject to revisions as from budget year 2018. Member states funding of Rural Development include statutory co-financing and national top-ups and exclude domestic policy.

Note by Turkey: The information in this document with reference to "Cyprus" relates to the southern part of the Island. There is no single authority representing both Turkish and Greek Cypriot people on the Island. Turkey recognises the Turkish Republic of Northern Cyprus (TRNC). Until a lasting and equitable solution is found within the context of the United Nations, Turkey shall preserve its position concerning the "Cyprus issue".

Note by all the European Union Member States of the OECD and the European Union: The Republic of Cyprus is recognised by all members of the United Nations with the exception of Turkey. The information in this document relates to the area under the effective control of the Government of the Republic of Cyprus.

Source: CAP 2014-20 Budget and OECD calculations based on national 2014-20 RDP budget as published in: http://ec.europa.eu/agriculture/rural-development-2014-2020/country-files/index_en.htm, 2016.

Figure 2.2. Ratio of public spending to the value of agricultural output

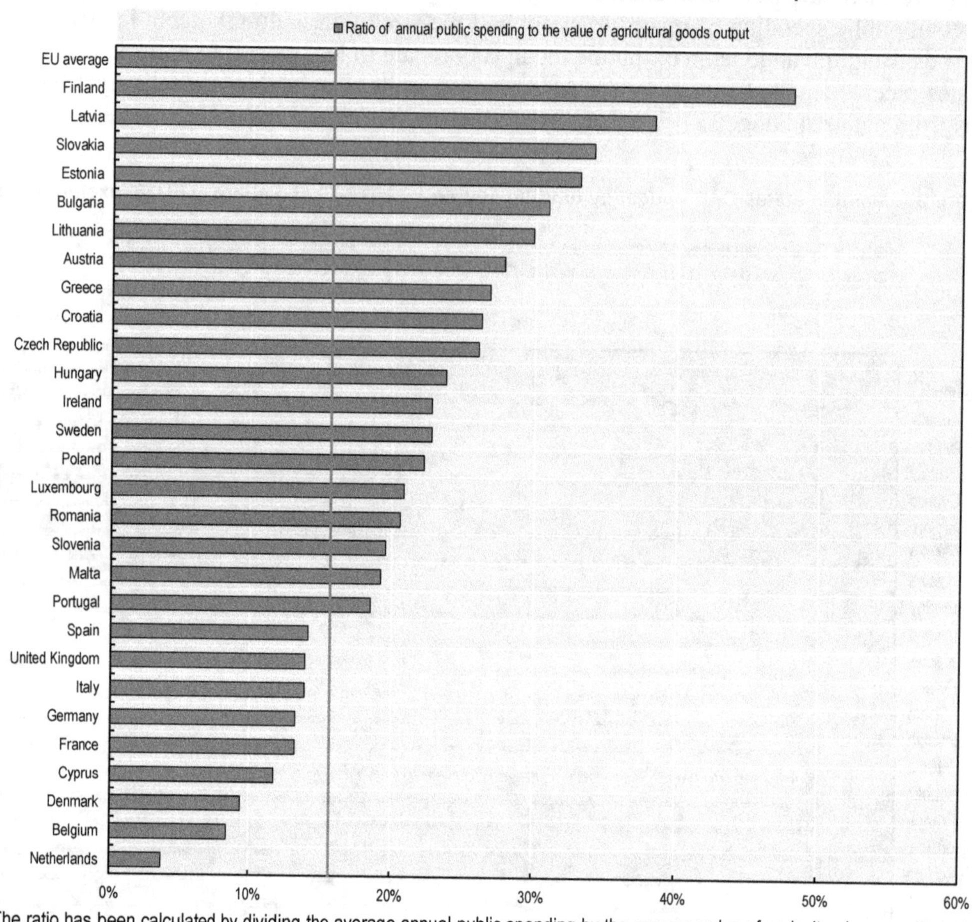

Note: The ratio has been calculated by dividing the average annual public spending by the average value of agricultural commodity output in 2014-16. Public spending includes member states statutory co-financing of Rural Development and national top-ups, and excludes domestic policy. Budgets represented are after transfers between pillars and may be subject to revisions as from budget year 2018.

Source: CAP 2014-20 Budget and OECD calculations based on national 2014-20 RDP budget as published in: http://ec.europa.eu/agriculture/rural-development-2014-2020/country-files/index_en.htm, 2016. Value of agricultural goods output: Eurostat, Economic Accounts for Agriculture database, agricultural goods output, production value at producer prices, February 2017.

Member states may use their national budget, in addition to the spending under the CAP, for specific national measures that target sectors or objectives, as long as they comply with the European Union's State Aid rules and do not distort competition within the common market (Box 2.1). These national measures are not covered in this report.

While in the past, transfers could only occur from pillar 1 to pillar 2, the CAP 2014-20 offers member states the flexibility to transfer monies both ways between pillars. The transfers are limited to 15% of their pillar 1 attributions, raised by another 10% for member states with an average payment per hectare that is less than 90% of the EU average payment per hectare, and 15% of pillar 2 attributions, raised by another 10% for twelve member states receiving less than 90% of the EU average direct payment per hectare allocation.[1] Eleven member states have chosen to transfer funds to the second pillar,[2] while five have transferred funds to the first pillar.[3] The net result is a larger pillar 2 budget for the European Union as a whole (i.e. net transfers from pillar 1 to pillar 2) (EC, 2016a). Member states may review their decisions in this regard by August 2017, for implementation of changes in 2018. Contrary to EAFRD (pillar 2) sourced budgets; member states are exempt from co-financing transfers from EAGF (pillar 1) to their pillar 2 budgets. Also new in the CAP 2014-20 is the so-called convergence that initiates the narrowing of the gap between per hectare payments both domestically (internal convergence) and across countries (external convergence).

Box 2.1. State Aid in the EU agricultural and forestry sectors and in rural areas

State aid and its conditions apply in all sectors and are not specific to agriculture.

Article 107 of the Treaty on the Functioning of the European Union (TFEU), defines State aid as "any aid granted by a Member State or through State resources in any form whatsoever which distorts or threatens to distort competition by favouring certain undertakings or the production of certain goods […], in so far as it affects trade between Member States" (OJ, 2012).

Although state aid is, in principle, prohibited, it can be authorised by the European Commission (EC) if it is found to be compatible with the internal market, according to compatibility scenarios laid down in the Treaty and compatibility criteria, predefined by the EC, for notifiable aid and block-exempted aid (by regulations). Under so-called block-exemption regulations for state aid, the Commission defines the conditions under which specific categories of State aid are compatible with the Treaty, thus exempting them from the requirement of prior notification and Commission approval. Such exemptions are associated to an obligation for member states to provide summaries of information concerning aid implemented. (OJ, 2015) Those summaries are published on the website of the Commission. Article 108 TFEU also sets out the main procedural principles governing the action to ensure member states' compliance with the substantive state aid rules.

In the agricultural sector, the difference between notified aid and the block-exempted aid lays within the scope of the beneficiaries. Block-exempted aid to agriculture is open to small and medium sized enterprises, while notified aid is open also to large enterprises though large enterprises have to prove the need for aid by presenting counterfactual scenario.

The state aid rules in the agricultural sector are based on three principles. They must follow the general principles of competition policy, be coherent and consistent with the EU's common agricultural and rural development policies and take into account the EU's international commitments.While Article 42 of the TFEU says that the state aid rules apply to production of and trade in agricultural products, the extent to which they apply is determined by the European Parliament and the Council who in Regulation 1308/2013 laid down that state aid rules should apply to agricultural products, with the exception of the market measures, direct payments and rural development measures in the CAP, which are exempted from state aid control.

Thus, all measures financed exclusively from national budgets, which fulfil the criteria are subject to state aid control. Guidelines were issued by the European Commission on the general criteria used when assessing the compatibility of aid with the internal market. They apply in case of notifiable aid. The cases are individually assessed and authorisation is granted when compatibility with the rules in the guidelines is established.

Regulation No 702/2014 (OJ, 2014) also allows the granting of certain categories of state aid to the agricultural sector, without prior notification to the European Commission, as the compatibility conditions are pre-defined for each category of aid included in the regulation.

All state aid cases that have been the object of a Commission decision since 1 January 2000 are available in the Commission's competition case database, including information on block-exemption cases registered by the Commission. It does not include information on on-going cases for which no decision has yet been taken.

Sources:
General information on EU State Aid: http://ec.europa.eu/competition/state_aid/scoreboard/index_en.html.
Compilation of EU State Aid rules in force: http://ec.europa.eu/competition/state_aid/legislation/compilation/index_en.html.
Competition cases database: http://ec.europa.eu/competition/elojade/isef/index.cfm?clear=1&policy_area_id=3.
Statistics on state aid expenditures in the EU agricultural and forestry sectors and in rural areas:
http://ec.europa.eu/eurostat/tgm_comp/table.do?tab=table&init=1&plugin=1&language=en&pcode=comp_ag_01.

Further information on state aid policy in agriculture, forestry and in rural areas: https://ec.europa.eu/agriculture/stateaid_en.

2.2. Overview of new features of the CAP 2014-20

Most new features of the CAP 2014-20 are in pillar 1. These include the budgetary provision for a Crisis reserve, the per hectare Greening payment, the mandatory Young farmer top-up and a number of choice schemes, including the sector (commodity) specific Voluntary Coupled Support payment, the additional payment to the first hectares also called the redistributive payment, the payment to Areas with Natural Constraints, the limits put on high levels of payments under degressivity and the small farm simplification scheme (Anania and Pupo D'Andrea, 2015).

While most measures under pillar 1 continue to apply across the board to all farms, the CAP 2014-20 offers member states more flexibility to tailor and target pillar 1 expenditures to support own objectives, while this has always been true for pillar 2 Rural Development Programmes (Box 2.2).

Box 2.2. Rural Development Programme priorities and measures

Rural Development is part of the EU-level Common Strategic Framework covering all support from European Structural and Investment (ESI) funds. The ESI brings together five funds; these include the European Agricultural Fund for Rural Development (EAFRD) the European Regional Development Fund (ERDF), the Cohesion Fund, the European Social Fund (ESF) and the European Maritime and Fisheries Fund (EMFF). These funds are implemented in member states through partnership agreements.

Rural Development, also known as pillar 2, has been reorganised from four thematic axes[1] in the CAP 2007-13 to six priorities. The six priority areas of pillar 2 of the CAP 2014-20 are as follows: 1) Fostering knowledge transfer and innovation; 2) Enhancing competitiveness of all types of agriculture and the sustainable management of forests; 3) Promoting food chain organisation, including processing and marketing, and risk management; 4) Restoring, preserving and enhancing ecosystems; 5) Promoting resource efficiency and the transition to a low-carbon economy; and 6) Promoting social inclusion, poverty reduction and economic development in rural areas. This last priority is also identified as LEADER (from the French *Liaison Entre Actions de Développement de l'Économie Rurale*).

Member states can choose from a menu of 20 measures to serve the priorities they have identified in their Rural Development Programmes. The list of measures available under the RDP is as follows:

M01	Knowledge transfer and information actions	M02	Advisory services, farm management and farm relief services	M03	Quality schemes for agricultural products and foodstuffs	M04	Investments in physical assets
M05	Restoring agricultural production potential damaged by natural disasters and catastrophic events and introduction of appropriate prevention actions	M06	Farm and business development	M07	Basic services and village renewal in rural areas	M08	Investments in forest area development and improvement of the viability of forests
M09	Setting-up of producer groups and organisations	M10	Agri-environment and climate	M11	Organic farming	M12	Natura 2000 and Water Framework Directive payments
M13	Payments to areas facing natural or other specific constraints	M14	Animal Welfare	M15	Forest environmental and climate services and forest conservation	M16	Co-operation
M17	Risk management	M18	Financing of complementary national direct payments for Croatia	M19	Support for LEADER local development	M20	Technical assistance
M113	Early retirement (outstanding from CAP 2007-13)	M131	Meeting standards based on Community legislation (outstanding from CAP 2007-13)				

Two conditions apply: a minimum 30% of rural development funding from the EU budget is spent on measures related to the environment and climate change adaptation, including forestry and investments in physical assets; and another 4% is spent on the LEADER approach. Previously 25% of the budget was to be allocated to environmental measures in the second Axis and it was required that each Axis receives at least 10% of the EU budget.

Member states may develop their RDP at national or regional levels to be implemented throughout the CAP 2014-20 lifespan. Six member states, Belgium, France, Germany, Italy, Spain, and the United Kingdom have developed regional RDP, while Finland and Portugal have made a distinction between their mainland and islands. Overall, 118 Rural Development Programmes were developed and implemented.

Member state choices as to which measures they implement determine how close to the producer and to the farm the programmes are delivered. These can support on-farm investment, services and insurance; they can also be paid based on area or animals, or be offered as support to the sector and sometimes to the wider rural area. When looking into member state choices, it is important to note that all member states have chosen to target at least 65% of their rural development budget to the farm, with some as high as 90% and more. On average 77% of pillar 2 funds result in a direct transfer to the farm (PSE) (Figure 2.3), while 6% goes to the agricultural sector and the remaining 17% to forestry or rural areas at large.

---

1. Rural Development under the CAP 2007-13 was organised under the following four Axes: Axis 1. Improving the competitiveness of the agricultural and forestry sector; Axis 2. Improving the environment and the countryside; Axis 3. Improving the quality of life in rural areas and encouraging diversification of the rural economy; Axis 4. Leader.

Figure 2.3. CAP Rural development budget classified using the OECD indicators of support - European Union 28

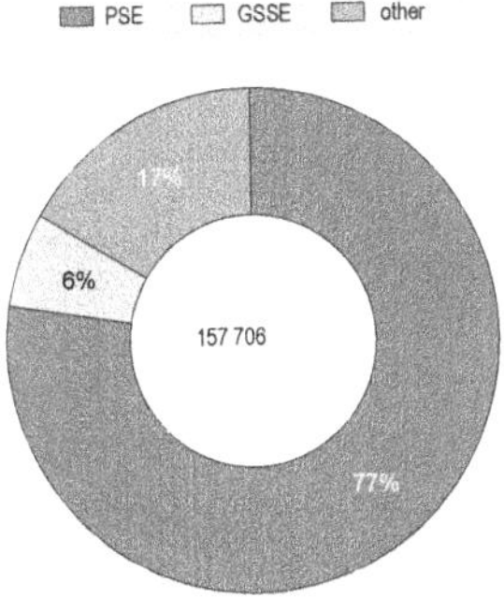

Source: OECD calculations based on national 2014-20 RDP budget as published in: http://ec.europa.eu/agriculture/rural-development-2014-2020/country-files/index_en.htm, 2016.

Figure 2.4 illustrates this classification by member states. In Denmark, Greece, Malta, Romania and Sweden more than 10% of RDP expenditure go to services to the sector by supporting education and advisory services as well as producer groups (GSSE). Portugal and Spain use more than 10% of RDP funds to support forestry, represented in the "other" category.

Figure 2.4. CAP rural development budget classified using the OECD indicators of support – Member states

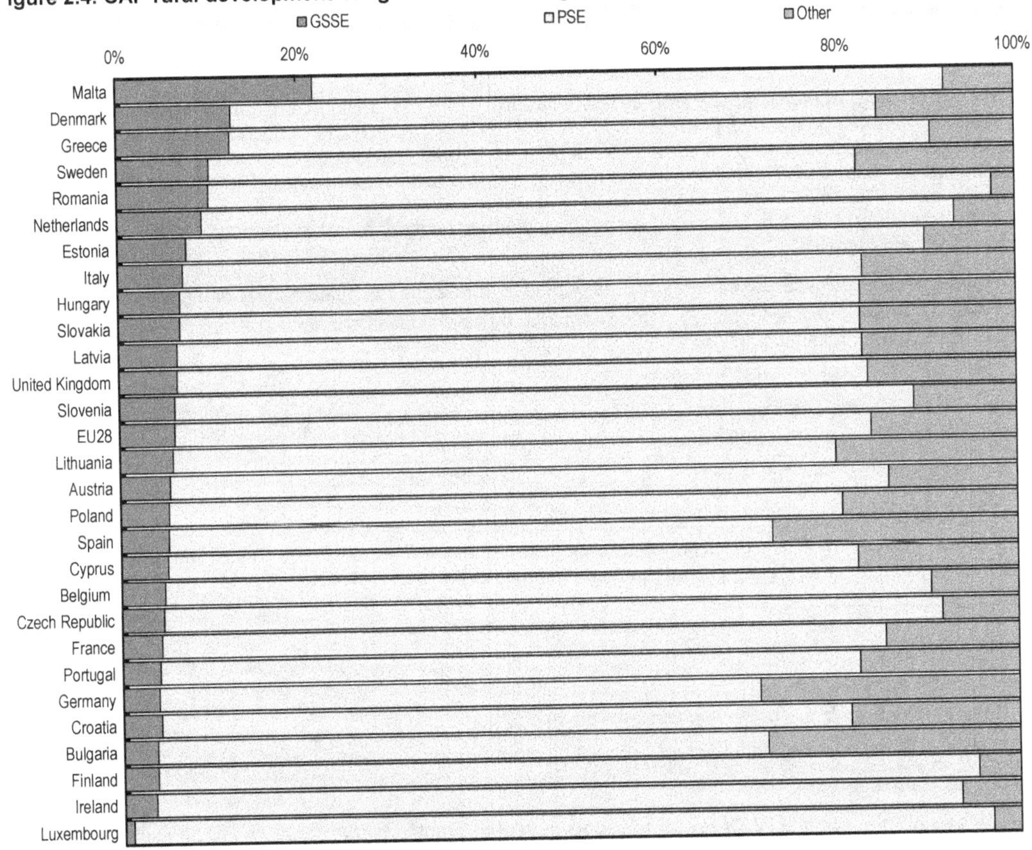

Countries are ranked according to the share of the GSSE in the rural development budget.
Source: OECD calculations based on national 2014-20 RDP budget as published in: http://ec.europa.eu/agriculture/rural-development-2014-2020/country-files/index_en.htm, 2016.

Main measures

The following section describes and discusses the most prominent features of the CAP 2014-20. In order to do so, the OECD framework of indicators of support is used to categorise the payments that result from the CAP 2014-20 (Box 2.3). Calculations published in the 2016 report *Agricultural Policy Monitoring and Evaluation* (OECD, 2016) are used. It is important to note that the calculations captured only those changes implemented in 2015. Pillar 2 measures of the CAP 2014-20 were not yet implemented at the time and they were not included in the report. Farm level and social impacts, such as rural development are not measured.

Box 2.3. Classification of the new measures of the CAP 2014-20

Policy measures included in the PSE are classified according to specific implementation criteria. These identify the economic features of policy measures, which have important consequences for the analysis of the potential impacts on production, income, consumption, trade, and the environment. Seven categories are used that identify the transfer basis for the policy, whether the basis is current or non-current, and whether production is required or not.

Policy measures that support producers collectively are included in the General Services Support Estimate (GSSE). They are classified into one of six main categories and related sub-categories according to the nature of the services provided to agriculture generally (and not to individual producers or consumers). More details on the OECD indicators of support are available in the PSE manual.

This box summarises the results of the application of the classification to the new measures under the CAP 2014-20. As shown in the table below new measures of the CAP relate to the B, C and E categories of the PSE and to the H and K categories of the GSSE. Current information available suggests that existing measures under categories A, D or F of the PSE and categories I, J, L or M of the GSSE are unchanged.

CAP 2014-20 measures that support producers individually (PSE)

A. Support based on commodity output: This category groups Transfers arising from policy measures that create a gap between domestic market prices and border prices (Market Price Support) and Transfers from taxpayers to agricultural producers from policy measures based on current output (Payments based on output)

B. Payments based on input use: Transfers from taxpayers to agricultural producers arising from policy measures based on on-farm use of inputs:

B.2. *Fixed capital formation*: Transfers reducing the on-farm investment cost of farm buildings, equipment, plantations, irrigation, drainage and soil improvements.

P2. M04.1	Investments in physical assets: improve the overall performance and sustainability of the agricultural holding
P2. M05	Restoring agricultural production potential damaged by natural disasters and catastrophic events and introduction of appropriate prevention actions
P2. M06	Farm and business development (see also J)

B.3. *On-farm services*: Transfers reducing the cost of technical, accounting, commercial, sanitary and phyto-sanitary assistance, and training provided to individual farmers.

P2. M02	Advisory services, farm management and farm relief services (see also H)
P2. M17	Risk management

C. Payments based on current A/An/R/I, production required: Transfers from taxpayers to agricultural producers arising from policy measures based on current area, animal numbers, receipts or income, and requiring production.

P1. DP.	Voluntary coupled support
P2. M10	Agri-environment and climate
P2. M11	Organic farming
P2. M12	Natura 2000 and Water Framework Directive payments
P2. M13	Payments to areas facing natural or other specific constraints
P2. M14	Animal Welfare

D. Payments based on non-current A/AN/R/I, production required: Transfers from taxpayers to agricultural producers arising from policy measures based on non-current (i.e. historical or fixed) area, animal numbers, receipts or income, with current production of any commodity required.

E. Payments based on non-current A/An/R/I, production not required: Transfers from taxpayers to agricultural producers arising from policy measures based on non-current (i.e. historical or fixed) area, animal numbers, receipts or income, with current production of any commodity not required but optional.

P1. DP.	Basic Payment Scheme
P1. DP.	Single Area Payment Scheme (SAPS, continued from previous CAP)
P1. DP.	Redistributive payment

P1. DP.	Greening
P1. DP.	Payments for areas with natural constraints
P1. DP.	Payments for young farmers
P1. DP.	Small farmers scheme

F. Payments based on non-commodity criteria: Transfers from taxpayers to agricultural producers arising from policy measures based on: *F.1. Long-term resource retirement, F.2. Specific non-commodity output F.3. Other non-commodity criteria.*

P2. M04.4	Investments in physical assets: non -productive investments linked to the achievement of agri- environment -climate objectives

G. Miscellaneous payments: Transfers from taxpayers to farmers for which there is insufficient information to allocate them to the appropriate categories.

CAP 2014-20 measures that support producers collectively (GSSE)

H. Agricultural knowledge and innovation system

H.2. Agricultural knowledge transfer: Budgetary expenditure to finance agricultural vocational schools and agricultural programmes at high education levels, generic training and advice to farmers (e.g. accounting rules, pesticide application), not specific to individual situations, and data collection and information dissemination networks related to agricultural production and marketing.

P2.M01	Knowledge transfer and information actions
P2.M02.3	Advisory services, farm management and farm relief services: promote the training of advisors (see also B)

I. Food inspection and control

J. Development and maintenance of rural infrastructure

J.1. Hydrological infrastructure: Budgetary expenditure financing public investments into hydrological infrastructure (irrigation and drainage networks).

P2. M04.3	Investments in physical assets: access to farm and forest land, land consolidation and improvement, and the supply and saving of energy and water

J.2. Storage, marketing and other physical infrastructure: Budgetary expenditure that finance investments to off-farm storage and other market infrastructure facilities related to handling and marketing primary agricultural products (silos, harbour facilities – docks, elevators; wholesale markets, futures markets), as well as other physical infrastructure related to agriculture when agriculture is the main beneficiary.

P2. M04.3	Investments in physical assets: access to farm and forest land, land consolidation and improvement, and the supply and saving of energy and water

J.3. Institutional infrastructure: Budgetary expenditure that finance investments to build and maintain institutional infrastructure related to the farming sector (e.g. land cadastres; machinery user groups, seed and species registries; development of rural finance networks; support to farm organisations, etc.).

P2. M16	Co-operation

J.4. Farm restructuring: Budgetary payments related to reform of farm structures that finance entry, exit or diversification (outside agriculture) strategies.

P2. M06.2	Farm and business development: diversify into non-agricultural activities in rural areas
P2. M06.4	Farm and business development: investments in creation and development of non-agricultural activities
P2. M06.5	Farm and business development: permanent transfer of small farm holdings

K. Marketing and promotion

K.1. Collective schemes for processing and marketing: Budgetary expenditures that finance investments in collective – mainly for primary processing – marketing schemes and marketing facilities, designed to improve the marketing environment for agriculture.

P2. M03	Quality schemes for agricultural products and foodstuffs: participation in quality schemes
P2. M04.2	Investments in physical assets: processing, marketing and/or development of agricultural products
P2. M09	Setting-up of producer groups and organisations

K.2. Promotion of agricultural products: Budgetary expenditure that finance assistance to collective promotion of agro-food products (e.g. promotional campaigns, participation in international fairs).

P2. M03	Quality schemes for agricultural products and foodstuffs: information and promotion activities

L. Cost of public stockholding

M. Miscellaneous

Notes: Category descriptions are reproduced as published in the PSE Manual. P1: pillar 1 measures. P2: pillar 2 measures. Measures may be categorised in several ways depending on their implementation. A/AN/R/I: Area planted, Animal number, Receipts, Income.
Source: Classification based on the *OECD PSE Manual* (OECD, 2016).

In the CAP 2014-20, the overall monetary transfers and the implementation modes are largely unchanged. Therefore, the structure of support as captured by the PSE has not changed with the new CAP. Where changes occur, they are mostly qualitative and do not depart from previous implementation modes, and consequently no changes are recorded in terms of the PSE framework. While the BPS, the SAPS, and other direct payments under pillar 1 are conditional to cross-compliance, more conditions are associated with the Greening payment. The PSE framework cannot accommodate nor interpret such a grading scale of conditions. Therefore, the BPS, the SAPS and the greening payments are classified under the same categories

The comparison suggests that the impact of the policy changes in CAP 2014-20 on production, prices, trade, welfare and the environment is likely to be small. This is confirmed when using the CAPRI model to estimate, *ex ante,* the impacts of new measures on production, prices, trade, welfare and the environment, as the model shows that the effects of the CAP 2014-20 would generally be minor at the aggregate level (Box 2.4).

Box 2.4. CAPRI model scenarios: assumptions and results

CAPRI is a simulation model of the agricultural sector with a detailed treatment of EU regions at the NUTS2 level using the FADN dataset (Pérez Domínguez et al., 2016). The simulations reported here were carried out with the CAPRI model for the simulation-year 2020 using a base year of 2008.[1] Budget data used for CAPRI includes pillar 1 and pillar 2 expenditure related to agriculture. It excludes parts of pillar 2 expenditure that are not agricultural specific. Within the overall national first pillar budgets and taking into account transfers between pillars, four scenarios were simulated that attempt to isolate different measures of the CAP 2014-20. Key scenario assumptions are listed in Annex Table 2.A1.1. Results are compared to a reference scenario representing the CAP 2007-13 as if continued up to year 2020.[2]

The four scenarios are as follows:

Scenario 1. CAP 2014-20 includes:

- Basic Payment Scheme based on the Single Farm Scheme of the reference period and a convergence formula
- Voluntary Coupled Support
- Greening: by applying the three conditions: Ecological Focus Area requirement, minimum restriction on Crop Diversification, a lower limit applies to the share of land that has to be permanent grass land
- Young farmer top-up

Scenario 2. No Voluntary Coupled Support (no-VCS): Voluntary Coupled Support is not allowed and the funds that were allocated to the VCS in scenario 1 flow into the Basic Payment Scheme instead.

Scenario 3. No-greening: Greening conditions are waived and the funds allocated to greening flow into the BPS instead. No Ecological Focus Area requirement, no minimum restriction on Crop Diversification, no lower limit on the share of land that has to be permanent grass land.

Scenario 4. Flat rate BPS: A single BPS rate per hectare is applied across regions within each country, while BPS rates remain different across countries.

Main results[3]

According to the CAPRI model results, the effects of the CAP 2014-20 show minor differences at EU28 aggregate level when compared to the reference scenario based on the continuation of the CAP 2007-13 (Table 2.2). A more detailed breakdown of results shows differences between country groupings, these are highlighted in Tables 2.3 and 2.4. When analysing the different scenarios, the results of the first (CAP 2014-20) and fourth (flat rate BPS) scenarios are very closely aligned, suggesting that, despite a smaller budget allocated to the BPS compared to the CAP 2007-13, the Basic Payment Scheme remains the main determinant of CAP impacts on production, prices, trade and welfare. The analysis of the different scenarios also suggests offsetting effects between the greening payment and the Voluntary Coupled Support in sectors where these payments have the largest impact. This, so-called, offsetting effect can be illustrated by the results of the no-greening and the no-VCS scenarios on agricultural area and set-aside described below. If no greening payments are made and funds used under the BPS the area under land set-aside would be reduced by 3% compared to the reference scenario. While, if no VCS are disbursed and other features of the CAP 2014-20 are implemented, land set-aside would be increased by nearly 12% compared to the reference scenario. Suggesting that area under land set-aside increases with greening while it is reduced with the VCS payment.

Compared to the reference scenario, the agricultural area under the CAP 2014-20 scenario shows minor differences (less than 0.5% variations) with few exceptions. The effects are mostly visible for cereals, pulses, set-aside and pasture (Annex Table 2.A1.2). Under scenario 1 (CAP 2014-20), areas under cereals are reduced by 2%, a much smaller (0.4%) reduction would occur if no greening conditions applied. The area under pulses is increased by 27%, the change would be limited to less than 2% if no Voluntary Coupled Support (VCS) were attributed. Areas under set-aside or pasture are increased by nearly 6% and 2% respectively. The area set-aside would be increased by nearly 12% if no VCS were attributed; on the contrary, it would be reduced by 3% if no greening conditions are applied. The area under pasture would increase by nearly 1.9% under all scenarios except if

---

greening was not applied, where there would be a decrease by 1.3%. The model results suggest that livestock numbers are very stable except for a 5% to 6% increase of the sheep and goat meat animals, depending on the scenario. The main explanation for this increase is to be found in the increase of agri-environmental and climate payments under pillar 2, these payments are frequently attributed to the sheep and goat meat sector. The increase would be slightly smaller in the no-VCS scenario.

The differences in area and livestock numbers noted above are generally less marked on production, suggesting that the changes occur in less productive segments, as could have been expected. In turn, prices react to the moderate changes in production. Where area and production drop, i.e. cereals, higher prices are expected, while the increased numbers and production of sheep and goat meat would depress prices by more than 6% (Annex Tables 2.A1.3 and 2.A1.4).

The CAPRI model calculates agricultural income as the sum of market income and support payments (Table 2.2) in year 2020. Despite a small decrease in support, the average agricultural income under the CAP 2014-20 would be mostly stable at EU28 aggregate level under all scenarios, a very minor increase would occur in the no-VCS scenario. In the latter, higher market income resulting from higher prices more than compensates for lower support (Table 2.2). In order to better understand the differences between member states, EU28 was disaggregated into two groupings and EU15 and EU13 are analysed separately[4] (Table 2.3). The results of the CAP 2014-20 scenario suggest that average agricultural income in the EU15 is slightly down compared to the reference scenario across all sectors as the decrease in support payments is larger than the increase in market income. In the no-VCS scenario the drop of agricultural income in EU15 would be more contained because higher prices would result in higher market incomes. This scenario yields both the largest increase in market incomes of all scenarios considered, and also the smallest drop in direct payments. The opposite picture emerges for the EU13 where the market income is slightly reduced and support payments increased and add to a larger total income. The redistribution of payments between the EU15 and the EU13 is explained by the convergence formula.

The CAPRI analysis also suggests a very moderate income distribution effect between sectors (Table 2.4). The change can be explained by the combination of internal convergence and the fact that funds previously distributed per hectare are used to finance a number of other measures. In the cereals sector, the decrease in support in most countries is not balanced by higher market income. While total income in the cereals sector decreases in the EU15, it increases in the EU13. In the ruminants sector, the fall in market incomes is more than compensated by the increase of support payments and the total income increases in all but three member states (Austria, Spain and Finland) (Annex Tables 2.A1.5 and 2.A1.6).

Table 2.2. CAPRI model results: Agricultural income, tax payer expenditures and consumer surplus (estimated results in year 2020)

	Reference EUR million	Absolute difference to reference scenario in EUR million			
		CAP 2014-20	No-VCS	No-greening	Flat rate BPS
Agricultural income EU28 (Gross Value Added plus support)	165 745	-739	1 005.9	-1 630	-707.8
Taxpayer expenditure European Union 28	55 630	-720	-396	-575	-716
Consumer surplus European Union 28	12 237 802	-98	-1 035	729	-132

Notes

1. The CAPRI analysis was carried out by Torbjörn Jansson (Swedish University of Agricultural Sciences), Peter Witzke (EuroCARE Bonn GmbH) and Alexander Gocht (Thünen Institute).

2. Documentation on assumptions and more tables can be found in Annex 2.A1.

3. In all tables presenting results, the numbers for the reference run are provided in absolute terms, whereas the other scenarios are reported as differences to the reference scenario.

4. Budget data used for CAPRI includes pillar 1 and pillar 2 expenditure related to agriculture. It excludes parts of pillar 2 expenditure that are not agricultural specific.

5. EU15 consists of Austria, Belgium, Denmark, Finland, France, Germany, Greece, Ireland, Italy, Luxembourg, the Netherlands, Portugal, Spain, Sweden and the United Kingdom. EU13 consists of Bulgaria, Croatia, Cyprus, Czech Republic, Estonia, Hungary, Latvia, Lithuania, Malta, Poland, Romania, Slovakia and Slovenia. It should be noted that the member state prices are tied together within the market model regions, while allowing the prices in EU15 and EU13 to react differently.

The modest decrease of the CAP 2014-20 budget compared to the reference scenario is captured in the decrease of taxpayer expenditure. When considering the distribution across countries the results are more contrasted reflecting member state contributions to the CAP budget (Annex Table 2.A1.7). Because the model projections in 2020 do not reach the ceiling values of the regulation, and result in a lower spending (Table 2.2).

Consumer surplus is stable on average in the EU28. This is mainly due to the fact that agricultural commodities make a very small share of consumer expenditure, which is mostly composed of non-agricultural goods.

Table 2.3. CAPRI model results: Agricultural income (estimated results in year 2020)

		Reference EUR million	Absolute difference to reference scenario in EUR million			
			CAP 2014-20	No-VCS	No-greening	Flat rate BPS
EU15 Total	Total income	143 200	-1 997	-717	-2 657	-1 972
	Market income	98 382	104	1 236	-694	126
	Direct payments	44 818	-2 101	-1 953	-1 963	-2 098
EU13 Total	Total income	22 636	1 257	1 727	1 025	1 263
	Market income	11 812	-127	165	-363	-121
	Direct payments	10 824	1 384	1 562	1 388	1 384

Table 2.4. CAPRI model results: Agricultural income for cereal and ruminant farms (estimated results in year 2020)

	Reference (million euro/year)			CAP 2014-20 absolute difference to reference scenario		
Cereals	Market income	Direct payments	Total income	Market income	Direct payments	Total income
European Union 28	4 777	16 039	20 815	962	-1 369	-407
European Union 15	3 504	11 691	15 194	646	-1 196	-551
European Union 13	1 430	4 348	5 778	311	-172	138
Ruminant						
European Union 28	25 665	4 475	30 141	-1 307	2 714	1 407
European Union 15	27 334	4 153	31 487	-702	1 646	944
European Union 13	-1 232	322	-910	-585	1 068	482

Nonetheless, the results highlight some redistribution that occurs between sectors and member states (CAPRI). Average farm incomes in the EU28 would hardly be affected. The effects of external convergence are visible as the average agricultural income in the EU15 is slightly down compared to the reference scenario across all sectors as the decrease in support payments is larger than the increase in market income. The opposite picture emerges for the EU13 where the market income is slightly reduced and subsidies increased and add to a larger total income. The model confirms that, in the absence of the Voluntary Coupled Support, market income would be moderately higher.

The CAPRI analysis also suggests a modest income distribution effect between sectors. This can be explained by two factors. First internal convergence and second, the reduction of the direct payments funds previously distributed to all farms per hectare of land, now allocated to a number of other measures. In the cereals sector, the decrease in support in most countries is not balanced by higher market income and the total income of the sector decreases. The opposite is found for the ruminants sector where, despite a fall in market incomes, total income increases in all but three member states (Austria, Spain and Finland) compared to the reference scenario (Annex Tables 2.A1.5 and 2.A1.6).

The analysis shows that the Basic Payment Scheme remains the main determinant of CAP impacts on production, prices, trade and welfare. The analysis also suggests that greening has a land redistribution effect across sectors and keeps livestock numbers and production in check; however in sectors where they apply, the overall effects of the VCS are in the opposite direction and sometimes of larger magnitude.

New measures in the CAP 2014-20

The next section offers a more detailed analysis of the new measures, following the structure of the categories of the PSE framework (Box 2.3). Where relevant and available, CAPRI model results related to those measures are also presented and discussed (Box 2.4 and Annex 2.A1)

CAP 2014-20 measures that support producers individually (PSE)

Support based on commodity output

Market measures represent less than 5% of the CAP 2014-20 budget.[4] Their nature is mostly unchanged from the previous CAP and they may be invoked under certain market conditions.[5] The scope of support to private storage has been expanded to more products, and private storage has been part of the responses deployed since 2014 to address over supply and lower farm prices (Box 3.3). An approximate EUR 400 million crisis reserve guarantee is set aside every year to be used in case of emergency situations. If used and depending on the modes of implementation, the crisis reserve could be classified in different categories of the PSE, some less market and production distorting than support based on commodity output. If unspent, it is reverted to the direct payments budget in pillar 1.

Payments based on input use

Pillar 2 of the CAP 2014-20 hosts the measures that support on-farm services and investment. These include investments to improve on-farm competitiveness and also participation in insurance schemes that are part of the risk management priority. These are discussed in greater detail in Chapter 3. On-farm services and investment account for 35% of EU RDP expenditure on average, while wide variations across countries exist and member states have used all the flexibility offered to them in this respect. In five member states, they represent less than 20% of their RDP budget, while four member states allocate 50% and more of their RDP funds to such measures. It should be noted that most member states have emphasised on-farm investment rather than services.

Payments based on current areas and animal numbers

Expanding on the previous coupled support scheme under Article 68, the new Voluntary Coupled Support (VCS) allocates a larger budget to more sectors.[6] The CAP 2014-20 regulation (OJ, 2013a) offers flexibility to member states to grant coupled support to sectors or regions where specific types of farming or specific agricultural sectors that are particularly important for economic, social or environmental reasons, undergo certain difficulties. They may be granted to the extent necessary to create an incentive to maintain current levels of production in the sectors or regions concerned.

Member states must fund the VCS from their direct payments budget, within defined ceilings and provisions in the regulation allow member states to review their decision related to coupled payments by August 2016. In line with the provisions, some member states have come forward with changes to come into effect for 2017 payments.

All member states (except Germany) opted for some form of the VCS (Annex Table 2.A2.1). The share of VCS in the national ceilings varies from 0.2% in Ireland and 0.5% in Luxembourg and the Netherlands to 57% in Malta (EC, 2016a). The average share for the 27 countries that attribute VCS is around 10% (Figure 2.5). The range of commodities included and the amount of payments also vary across countries (Annex Table 2.A2.1).

Figure 2.5. Share of VCS in pillar 1 Direct Payments budget (% in 2015)

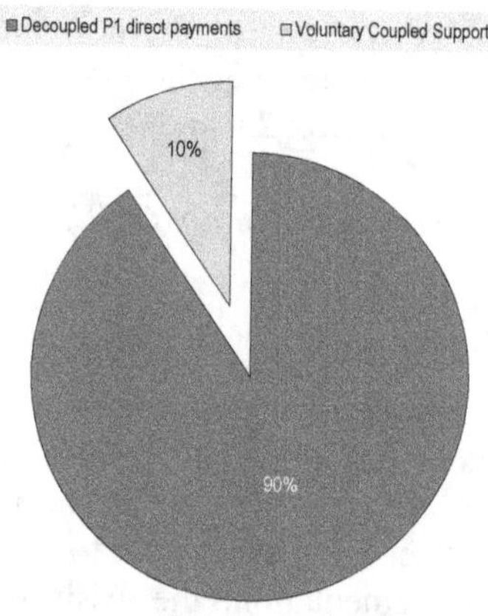

Source: DG Agriculture and Rural Development, European Commission, Voluntary Coupled Support, Decisions notified to the Commission by 1 August 2014, published 29 July 2015 (EC, 2016a).

Most of the VC support goes to beef and veal (41% of VCS), dairy (20%), sheep and goats (12%) and protein crops (11%). These commodities total 84% of total VCS. The remaining support is allocated to the following commodities: fruits and vegetables (5%), sugar beet (4%), cereals (2%), olive oil (2%), rice (1%) and a range of commodities with a share close to 0% (flax, grain legumes, hemp, hops, nuts, oilseeds, seeds, silkworms and starch potatoes) (Table 2.5).

Table 2.5. Sector share of total VCS

	Share of total VCS
Beef and veal	41%
Cereals	2%
Flax	0%
Fruit and vegetables	5%
Grain legumes	0%
Hemp	0%
Hops	0%
Milk and milk products	20%
Nuts	0%
Oilseeds	0%
Olive oil	2%
Protein crops	11%
Rice	1%
Seeds	0%
Sheep meat and goat meat	12%
Silkworms	0%
Starch potato	0%
Sugar beet	4%

Source: DG Agriculture and Rural Development, European Commission, Voluntary Coupled Support, Decisions notified to the Commission by 1 August 2014, published 29 July 2015.

Results of the CAPRI model indicate that, compared to the reference scenario, the VCS increases the allocation of land and herd size to supported sectors as farmers' production choices respond to policy incentives associated with coupled support (Table 2.6). Under the CAP 2014-20 scenario, the area under pulses is increased by 27% while the change would be limited to an increase by less than 2% if no VCS were attributed. The results also show that under the no-VCS scenario, the area under set-aside and fallow land would increase by 12%. As detailed in Annex 2.A.1, the reference scenario continues the CAP 2007-13 to year 2020, including its coupled support under Article 68. The results above compare the reference scenario to a CAP 2014-20 with no-VCS and attribution of the payments to the BPS.

This may bring to light contradicting signals received by farmers: on the one hand if there were no-VCS as part of the CAP 2014-20 more land would be set-aside or left fallow compared to the reference scenario. At the same time, the Ecological Focus Area (EFA) condition of the greening payment aims to encourage this same change. Except for sheep and goats, the model shows that if VCS are not allowed, production would decline and prices would rise, with a net positive effect on overall agricultural income.

The effects of the VCS on land-use and animal numbers were also underlined by evidence presented in a report analysing member state implementation of the CAP 2014-20 where environmentally valuable permanent grassland was brought into production as a result of the use of VCS to support livestock and crop production. In this case, the report highlights the fact that CAP implementation choices with regards to farm income and the environment and climate "have the potential to lead to RDP funds being used to counteract the effects of the decisions made under pillar 1." (EC, 2016b).

The effects on trade of the no-VCS scenario are generally moderate, except for exports of sheep and goat meat (up by nearly 9%) and cereals and oilseeds (down by 1.5% and 2.2% respectively). The effects of the no-VCS on imports are much smaller, as illustrated by the 0.6% increase of imports of the group other arable crops, the largest change in imports reported.

Table 2.6. CAPRI results of the no-VCS scenario

(% change as compared to reference)

Activity	Hectare and herd size	Production	Producer prices	Trade	
				Import	Export
Utilised agricultural area	0.10	Na	na	na	na
Cereals	-1.80	-1.30	1.30	0.30	-1.50
Oilseeds	-0.60	-0.50	0.70	-0.20	-2.20
Other arable crops	0.90	-0.80	0.60	0.60	0.90
- of which pulses	1.60	na	na	na	na
Vegetables and permanent crops	0.00	0.00	0.30	0.00	-0.10
Fodder activities	0.30	na	na	na	na
Set-aside and fallow land	11.60	na	na	na	na
Meat	na	-0.10	0.50	0.20	0.00
All ruminants	-0.60	na	na	na	na
All cattle activities	-1.30	na	na	na	na
All dairy	-0.60	na	na	na	na
Other animals	0.60	na	na	na	na
Beef meat activities	-2.70	-1.10	2.30	0.20	-0.70
- Pork meat	na	0.00	0.10	0.10	0.00
- Sheep and goat meat	na	4.80	-5.30	-0.30	8.80
- Poultry meat	na	-0.20	0.30	0.40	-0.20
Other animal products	na	-0.20	0.10	0.20	0.30
- Raw milk	na	0.00	0.00	0.00	0.10
- Eggs	na	-0.10	0.30	0.30	-0.20
Pasture	1.90	na	na	na	na
Arable land	-0.70	na	na	na	na

Note: na: not applicable.

Source: CAPRI model results, 2016.

Other payments based on current area and animal numbers that require production are sourced in pillar 2. These consist of the Agri-environment and climate measures, support to organic farming and support to enhance Animal welfare. Pillar 2 also delivers support to compensate for income disparities in Areas with Natural Constraints and areas under Natura 2000 and the Water Framework Directive. These measures are described in greater detail as part of the review of environmental measures in Chapter 4.

Payments based on non-current criteria

The bulk of CAP support is delivered as payments based on area entitlement where the level of payments is based on non-current (historical) criteria. This support is provided through the Basic Payment Scheme (BPS) and the Single Area Payment Scheme (SAPS). Member states who apply the BPS[7] may choose to do so at national or regional level, in the latter case uniform per hectare payment rates apply at regional level.[8] As compared with its predecessor, the SPS, the gap in per hectare payment rates under the BPS should be narrowed across regions under internal convergence.[9] The SAPS applies in all but three new member states.[10] It offers a uniform per hectare payment rate. External convergence would slightly close the gap between average per-hectare payment rates across countries by 2019. Payments under the BPS and the SAPS are expected to have less influence on production decisions as they are disbursed to eligible hectares and do not require production. A novelty in the CAP 2014-20 is that part of the overall budget of the BPS is diverted to fund a number of new choice or compulsory schemes. As a result, in 2015, about 55% of the direct payments budget was disbursed on average by member states under the BPS or the SAPS, compared to the CAP 2007-13, where the SPS used 74% of the direct payments budget in 2014 (Figure 2.6). Member states used the remaining 45% to fund other compulsory and choice measures.

Figure 2.6. The Basic Payment Scheme and the Single Area Payment Scheme as a share of direct payments (pillar 1) – 2015

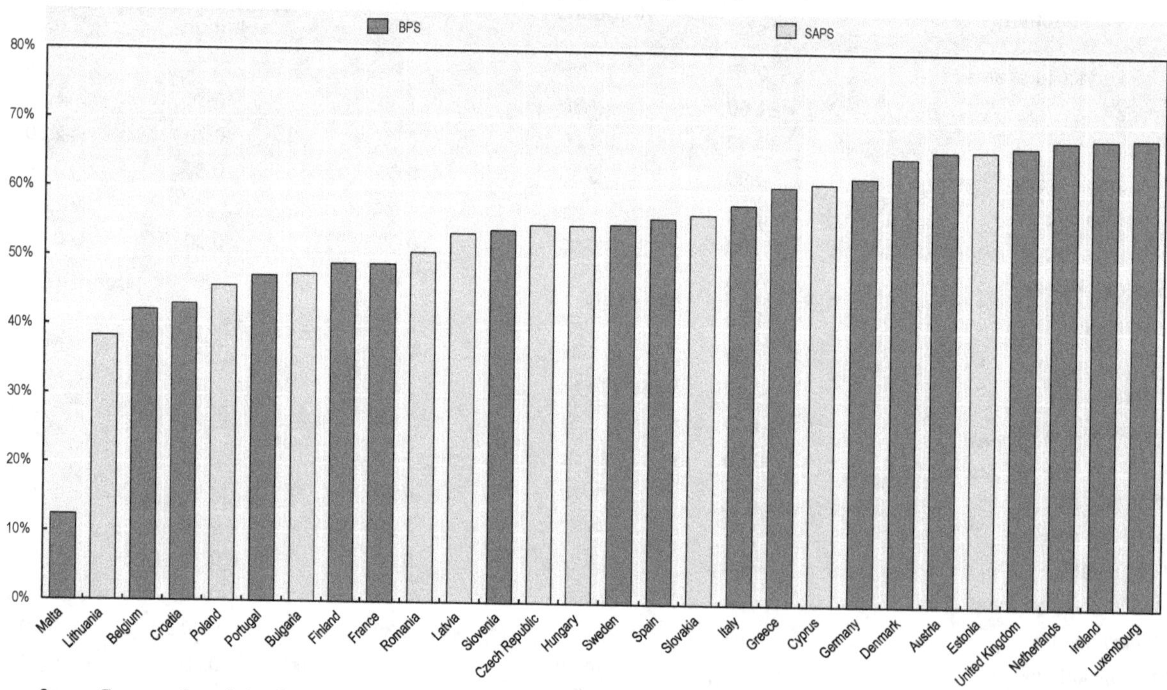

Source: European Commission Direct payments post 2014, Decisions taken by member states by 1 August 2014 (EC, 2016a).

The Greening payment is compulsory and, by far, the most important of these schemes from a budgetary point of view. The Young farmer payment is the other compulsory scheme. Choice measures include the Voluntary Coupled Support (VCS), the conditions of the redistributive payment, the small farmer scheme and the payment to Areas with Natural Constraints. CAPRI model scenarios projections of the BPS and Greening in year 2020 are shown in Table 2.7. They mainly illustrate the expected effects of convergence and the higher per hectare payments that would result if no VCS were allowed, and the fact that average per hectare payments would be mostly stable in the other scenarios.

Thirty per cent of the direct payments budget is allocated to the Greening payment. The implementation of this scheme is similar to that of the BPS and of the SAPS and the additional conditions associated are not captured by the PSE framework. The CAPRI model results show that Greening influences crop choices and herd sizes, however it is likely to have small aggregate impacts except on some specific land allocations. The effects of greening on land use result from the EFA and also from the obligation to maintain permanent grassland. These changes are passed onto production, with more visible changes in smaller sectors, such as field crops other than cereals and oilseeds and sheep and goat meat. As a result of the greening payment, agricultural prices are higher and consumer surplus reduced. Chapter 4 offers a detailed review of this measure.

Table 2.7. CAPRI results: Average payments per hectare as sum of basic payment, greening supplement and Single Area Payment where applicable

(EUR/ha)

Country	CAP 2014-20	No-VCS	No-greening	Full flat rate
Belgium	250	306	251	250
Denmark	278	287	279	278
Germany	253	253	253	252
Austria	214	218	215	214
Netherlands	364	366	364	364
France	159	198	160	159
Portugal	134	168	134	134
Spain	178	204	179	179
Greece	289	323	290	290
Italy	229	258	230	229
Ireland	282	283	282	282
Finland	187	227	187	187
Sweden	202	232	203	202
United Kingdom	189	192	189	189
Czech Republic	181	213	181	181
Estonia	145	149	148	145
Hungary	187	219	188	187
Lithuania	118	144	120	118
Latvia	118	139	121	118
Poland	148	176	149	148
Slovenia	222	262	222	222
Slovak Republic	173	197	173	173
Croatia	142	172	143	142
Cyprus	258	282	262	258
Malta	160	407	160	160
Bulgaria	112	134	113	112
Romania	103	123	103	103

Source: CAPRI model results, 2016.

Nine member states chose to allocate higher payment rates to the first hectares under the so-called redistributive payment (Table 2.8).[11] Member states were given flexibility to offer these payments to either a maximum of 30 hectares or the average farm size, resulting in wide variations across countries; average farm size varies from 3 to 54 hectares. Different amounts can be paid per pre-defined tranches of hectares as long as the tranches apply identically to all farmers. Member states may review their decision to implement the redistributive payment and its conditions in any year. Like the BPS and the SAPS, the redistributive payment is not related to any productive activity, however it may add inertia to land transition and restructuring as it attaches a higher "rent" to these lands (EC, 2016c).

The Young Farmer payment is a new compulsory scheme under pillar 1. It supports the entry into the sector of farmers below the age of 40 with additional payments based on direct payment entitlement. A choice measure under pillar 2 of the CAP 2007-14 supported the entry in the sector of young. This pillar 2 support programme is continued in the CAP 2014-20 as part of the second element of the farm competitiveness priority. While the young farmer scheme in the first pillar results in a top up to the per hectare payment, support in the second pillar may take different forms, from on-farm investments to knowledge and advisory services and support for co-operation (Table 2.9).

Payments based on non-commodity criteria

In the past, EU member states have used a small portion of the rural development budget for agri-environmental measures to support the use of farm resources for non-commodity outputs. These activities or practices go beyond requirements and can include a wide variety of outputs such as biodiversity conservation or the creation and upkeep of specific landscape elements. At this point, it is unclear whether these payments are continued and integrated in the member states RDP or if budgets are used for other policy choices.

Table 2.8. The Redistributive payment as additional support to the first hectares (as percentage of national ceiling)

	2015	2016	2017	2018	2019	2020	Threshold supported (ha)	Avg. farm size (ha)
Belgium (Wallonia)	17	17	17	17	17	17	30	54
Bulgaria	7.1	7.1	7.1	7	7	7	30	6
Croatia	10	10	10	10	10	10	20	5.9
France	5.0	10	10	20	20	20	52	52
Germany	7	7	7	7	7	7	First tranche up to 30 Second tranche from 30.1 to 46	46
Lithuania	15	15	15	15	15	15	30	12
Poland	8.3	8.3	8.5	8.6	8.6	8.	First tranche up to 3 Second tranche from 3.1 to 30	6
Portugal	-	-	2.8	2.7	2.7	2.7	5	2.7
Romania	5.2	5.3	5.4	5.3	5.3	5.5	First tranche up to 5 Second tranche from 5.1 to 30	3
United Kingdom (Wales)	0.5	1.0	1.5	1.5	2.0	2.5	54	2.7

Notes: The ceilings and percentage foreseen may be changed on a yearly basis. Numbers for Belgium (Wallonia) are expressed at regional level.
Source: European Commission Redistributive payment, November 2016, https://ec.europa.eu/agriculture/sites/agriculture/files/ds-dp-redistributive-payment_en.pdf (accessed February 2017), and Government of Wallonia.

Table 2.9. Member states take up of the Young Farmer priority in pillar 2

(EUR million)

	Knowledge	Advisory services	Investments in physical assets	Farm and business development	Cooperation	Share in total RDP expenditure
Austria	8	1		90	0	1%
Belgium	10	10		98		7%
Bulgaria	2	1	21	77		3%
Croatia	2	2		50		2%
Cyprus			10	7		7%
Czech Republic	0			30		1%
Estonia	1	0		22		2%
Finland	3			145		2%
France	10	30	38	1 135	3	7%
Greece				308		5%
Hungary	7	3	125	122		6%
Ireland			120		2	3%
Italy	50	33	836	929	11	9%
Latvia				14		1%
Lithuania	1	0		65		3%
Luxembourg				8		2%
Malta		0	1	4		4%
Poland				718		5%
Portugal	1	3		214		5%
Romania	6	31		445		5%
Slovakia	1	0	18	30		2%
Slovenia	1			61		6%
Spain	14	6	136	676	20	6%
Sweden				16		0%
United Kingdom	4	3		33	1	1%
EU28	120	123	1 304	5 296	37	4%

Source: OECD calculations based on national 2014-20 RDP budget as published in: http://ec.europa.eu/agriculture/rural-development-2014-2020/country-files/index_en.htm, 2016.

CAP 2014-20 measures that support producers collectively (GSSE)

Agricultural knowledge transfer

Rural development measures that support Agricultural knowledge transfer and advisory services are continued. In the CAP 2014-20, support to knowledge transfer has been used across the board to support all pillar 2 priorities and on average member states have devoted 2%, and up to 6%, of their pillar 2 budgets to these services (Table 2.10). It should be noted that this percentage only covers expenditure on agricultural knowledge transfers from the RD budgets, and member states may use other education and advisory related budgets to cover related expenditure.

Table 2.10. Member state expenditure on Knowledge transfer and Advisory services

(EUR million)

	Knowledge transfer	Advisory services	Total RDP expenditure	Share in RDP expenditure
Austria	116	22	7 812	2%
Belgium	38	21	1 579	4%
Bulgaria	25	20	2 918	2%
Croatia	13	21	2 383	1%
Cyprus	2		243	1%
Czech Republic	3	4	3 074	0%
Denmark	37		907	4%
Estonia	12	9	993	2%
Finland	80	34	8 325	1%
France	171	131	16 985	2%
Germany	139	596	16 886	4%
Greece	78	162	5 880	4%
Hungary	54	45	4 174	2%
Ireland	126	8	3 916	3%
Italy	247	333	20 925	3%
Latvia	33	10	1 532	3%
Lithuania	23	5	1 978	1%
Luxembourg			368	0%
Malta	6	3	130	6%
Netherlands	35	30	1 645	4%
Poland	58	75	13 513	1%
Portugal	31	34	4 721	1%
Romania	67	71	9 473	1%
Slovakia	14	4	2 080	1%
Slovenia	13	11	1 107	2%
Spain	148	219	13 155	3%
Sweden	129	86	4 300	5%
United Kingdom	170	87	7 626	3%
EU28	1 868	2 041	158 627	2%

Source: OECD calculations based on national 2014-20 RDP budget as published in: http://ec.europa.eu/agriculture/rural-development-2014-2020/country-files/index_en.htm, 2016.

Marketing and promotion

Promoting food chain organisations is continued in the CAP 2014-20. Besides offering direct support to the setup of such organisations, this is also achieved by giving these organisations more visibility and a more prominent role. This was the case when compensation payments to fruit and vegetables producers related to the Russian embargo that was imposed in 2014 on imports from the European Union were doubled should a farmer place a claim through a producer organisation.

2.3. Future steps

After years of continuous and progressive reform, the new measures introduced by the CAP 2014-20 may be seen as an attempt to offer member states more flexibility to adapt a common set of policies to their own conditions by using the choice elements of the CAP, while at the same time adding more uniformity through the internal and external convergence of per hectare payments. Member states have embraced to varying degrees the increased flexibility and at this point in time it is unclear how these measures are combined and tailored to support CAP objectives as regards farm productivity and income.

Evidence should be collected to facilitate the evaluation of such flexibility and uniformity in enabling the agricultural sector to take up the challenge of improving productivity sustainably. This should be the focus of the on-going reflection on the future of the CAP.

Notes

1. The ceiling of transfers between Pillars is raised to 25% for Bulgaria, Estonia, Finland, Latvia, Lithuania, Poland, Portugal, Romania, Slovakia, Spain, Sweden and the United Kingdom.

2. Belgium, the Czech Republic, Denmark, Estonia, France, Germany, Greece, Latvia, the Netherlands, Romania, and the United Kingdom.

3. Croatia, Hungary, Malta, Poland and Slovakia.

4. However, the share of the support based on commodity output, which includes market price support and direct payments based on output represents 24% of the EU28 PSE and accounts for 4.4% of farm receipts on average in 2013-15.

5. The measures include: measures against market disturbance (art. 219 CMO); measures concerning animal diseases and loss of consumer confidence (art. 220 CMO); measures to resolve specific problems (art. 221 CMO); and measures concerning agreements and decisions during periods of severe imbalance in markets (art. 222 CMO) (OJ, 2013b).

6. Coupled support may be granted to the following sectors and production: cereals, oilseeds, protein crops, grain legumes, flax, hemp, rice, nuts, starch potato, milk and milk products, seeds, sheep meat and goat meat, beef and veal, olive oil, silkworms, dried fodder, hops, sugar beet, cane and chicory, fruit and vegetables and short rotation coppice (OJ, 2013a).

7. The BPS is applied in Slovenia, Malta and Croatia in addition to the EU15.

8. This is in accordance to Article 23 of Regulation (EU) No 1307/2013 establishing rules for direct payments. The regionalisation of the BPS is applied by Greece, Spain, Finland, Germany, France, and within two regions of the United Kingdom (England and Scotland).

9. A uniform per hectare rate payment for the BPS is delivered as from 2015 in Germany, France-Corsica, Malta, and the United Kingdom-England, and will be delivered by 2019 in Austria, the Netherlands, Finland, and the United Kingdom-Scotland and Wales, and by 2020 in Sweden. The other member states have opted for "partial convergence" by 2020. By that date, no payments should fall below 60% of the member states' average per hectare payment. Greece, Spain, France (except Corsica), Croatia, Italy, Portugal, Slovenia and Belgium have opted to limit the reduction in the unit value of payment entitlements that are above average to a maximum of 30% of their initial unit value.

10. The SAPS is applied in Cyprus, Czech Republic, Estonia, Hungary, Latvia, Lithuania, Poland, Slovakia, Bulgaria, and Romania. The BPS is applied in Slovenia, Malta, and Croatia in addition to the EU15.

11. The decision to implement the redistributive payment can be taken by member states in any year, and the percentage foreseen modified. In addition to the first eight member states or regions that apply the redistributive payment: Belgium-Wallonia, Bulgaria, Croatia, Germany, France, Lithuania, Poland, Romania and the United Kingdom-Wales, as of 2017, Portugal will also apply the redistributive payment. Bulgaria, Germany and Lithuania implemented the redistributive payment already in 2014.

References

Anania, G. and M.R. Pupo D'Andrea (2015), "The 2013 Reform of the Common Agricultural Policy", *The Political Economy of the 2014-2020 Common Agricultural Policy, An Imperfect Storm*, CEPS.

EC (2016a), Direct payments 2015-2020 Decisions taken by Member States by 1 August 2014 - State of play as at June 2016 - Information note, European Commission, Brussels, https://ec.europa.eu/agriculture/sites/agriculture/files/direct-support/direct-payments/docs/simplementation-decisions-ms-2016_en.pdf

EC (2016b), "Mapping and analysis of the implementation of the CAP", Directorate-General for Agriculture and Rural Development, European Commission, Brussels, https://ec.europa.eu/agriculture/sites/agriculture/files/external-studies/2016/mapping-analysis-implementation-cap/fullrep_en.pdf

EC (2016c), Redistributive payment, November 2016, https://ec.europa.eu/agriculture/sites/agriculture/files/ds-dp-redistributive-payment_en.pdf (accessed February 2016).

OECD (2016), "OECD's Producer Support Estimate and related indicators of agricultural support, Concepts, Calculations, Interpretation and Use (The PSE Manual)", Paris, www.oecd.org/tad/agricultural-policies/full%20text.pdf.

OECD (2011), *Evaluation of Agricultural Policy Reforms in the European Union*, OECD Publishing, Paris, http://dx.doi.org/10.1787/9789264112124-en.

Official Journal of the European Union (OJ) (2015), Council Regulation (EU) 2015/1588 of 13 July 2015 on the application of Articles 107 and 108 of the Treaty on the Functioning of the European Union to certain categories of horizontal State aid (codification)

OJ (2014), Commission Regulation (EU) No 702/2014 of 25 June 2014 declaring certain categories of aid in the agricultural and forestry sectors and in rural areas compatible with the internal market in application of Articles 107 and 108 of the Treaty on the Functioning of the European Union, Brussels.

OJ (2013a), Regulation (EU) No 1307/2013 of the European Parliament and of the Council establishing rules for direct payments to farmers under support schemes within the framework of the common agricultural policy, Brussels.

OJ (2013b), Regulation (EU) No 1308/2013 of the European Parliament and of the Council establishing a common organisation of the markets in agricultural products, Brussels.

OJ (2012), "Consolidated Version of the Treaty on the Functioning of the European Union", Official Journal of the European Union, C 326, 26 October 2012, http://eur-lex.europa.eu/resource.html?uri=cellar:41f89a28-1fc6-4c92-b1c8-03327d1b1ecc.0007.02/DOC_1&format=PDF.

Pérez Domínguez, I. et al. (2016), "Brief overview of the CAPRI modelling approach", *An Economic Assessment of GHG Mitigation Policy Options for EU Agriculture (EcAMPA 2)*, JRC Science for Policy Report, EUR 27973 EN, 10.2791/843461.

Annex 2.A1

CAPRI model scenario assumptions and selected result tables

Scenario assumptions

The simulations reported here were carried out with the CAPRI model for the simulation year 2020 using a base year of 2008. Four scenarios with variations of the CAP 2014-20 were simulated, and compared to a reference scenario representing the CAP up to 2013 as if continued up to 2020. Table 2.A1.1 summarises the key policy elements of the reference scenario and the CAP 2014-20.

In particular, the CAP 2014-20 scenario contained the following elements:

- A **Basic Payment Scheme** (BPS) which defines a payment per hectare of eligible land per farm (Individual Unit Values, IUV) based on single farm payments in the reference run and a convergence formula. Each country, even each arbitrary region within a country, can have a different convergence formula. The details on national and regional decisions were provided by the commission. **Convergence** of regional average IUV towards a narrowing corridor defined by several parameters was implemented in a way analogous to the regulation: the payment *region*, i.e. the sets of regions within which all farms share one convergence model (e.g. all grassland dominated farms in Greece, different models for Scotland and Wales in the United Kingdom etc.), the convergence model (linear or proportional adjustment of payments outside of the corridor), invocation of the so-called 30-percent-rule that may prevent IUVs to be reduced by more than 30%, target value of tunnel model (share of average IUV to converge to), share of gap to target IUV that is to be covered by the end of the convergence period, and the final year of the convergence process. The real policy is defined for individual farms and sometimes for regions that cannot be reproduce exactly in CAPRI. Policy was mapped to the closest resolution available in the model, which meant aggregations of NUTS2-regions.

- **Voluntary Coupled Support** (VCS). Each member state is permitted to couple up to 13% of the national first pillar budget to certain sectors. Details on national choices were provided to the modelling team by the commission, and used to define coupled subsidies per animal or hectare. In particular, all countries except Germany coupled some subsidies to beef sector. Also dairy, sheep and goat, and protein crops receive substantial amounts of subsidies.

- **Greening**. 30% of the pillar 1 budget was made conditional upon compliance with three basic rules:

  - set-aside of at least 5% (which may be exaggerated given various exceptions and flexibilities, see the technical annex) of the arable land

  - preventing a decrease in the area of grassland from the area in year 2013 (see notes in annex)

  - maintaining a minimum level of crop diversity at the NUTS2 level as measured by entropy of NUTS2 crop shares.

The set-aside requirement could be satisfied by allocating arable land to certain idling activities with low costs and no yield, but that enter the land balance of the farm and are eligible for Basic Payments. The minimum crop diversity requirement for NUTS2 regions was found by solving a farm-level optimization problem minimizing squared deviations from historical crop shares while complying with the crop diversity requirements of the regulation. Farm level results were then aggregated to NUTS2-level and the resulting change in NUTS2 level entropy was calculated.

- A **young farmer** top-up, crop specific coupled support to cotton, complementary national direct payments, a redistributive payment to the first hectares of each farm, and a first pillar payment to areas with natural constraints in only Denmark (other countries opting for keeping that in pillar 2).

Table 2.A1.1. Key scenario assumptions

	Reference	CAP 2014-20
National first pillar budget	As in Council Regulation No 73/2009	As in Regulation No 1307/2013
Transfers between pillars	None	As reported by member states to the European Commission
Payment entitlements for Single farm payments and Basic payment scheme	A number of entitlements defined, above which the marginal SFP is zero.	A number of entitlements defined, above which the marginal Basic Payment is zero.
Coupled support	Coupling of suckler cow payments in AT, FR, PT, ES, EL. Coupling of sheep and goat payments in ES, PT, DK and FI. Implementation of coupled support to various sectors as permitted under article 68 as reported by the commission.	As reported by the member states to the European Commission (all countries couple some support, in particular to beef, except Germany). Crop specific coupled support as in Art 58 of Regulation 1307/2013
Set-aside rate (share of area that has to be left fallow with minimum requirements)	None	5% ecological focus area
Crop diversification	None	Minimum diversity required, computed for each region based on micro-level simulations.
Grass land share in total land	No specific requirement	No decrease beyond 2013 levels

In the three partial reform scenarios, the CAP 2014-20 was modified as follows:

No-VCS: No voluntary coupled support permitted. The funds that were allocated to VCS in CAP 2014-20 flow into the Basic Payment Scheme instead.

No-Greening: No Ecological Focus Area requirement, no minimum restriction on Crop Diversity, no lower limit on the share of land that has to be permanent grassland. The funds allocated to greening are paid to farmers as a top up to BPS, but without the greening conditions attached.

Full flat rate: All countries let the BPS rates per hectare level out across regions (and farms, farm level is not simulated in this study) to become equal in all regions within each country but different across countries.

With regards to taxpayer expenditure, the model assumption is that the budget in CAP 2014-20 is not spent fully: (i) in the "no-VCS" scenario: the coupled support budget is not fully spent as the threshold on animal numbers or hectares exceeds the existing numbers (according to the model assumptions). By removing the VCS condition, the restriction on production is removed and the money is transferred to the Basic Payment, therefore the budget is spent in full; (ii) for the "no-greening" scenario several shifts occur. While these are small, the dominant effect for the EU as an aggregate, is that without greening some grassland turns into arable land. This leads to shifts in several payments in both directions. One of them is that previously unspent second pillar budget tied to arable cropping is now spent. There is uncertainty as to whether this particular effect is realistic, as it depends on details of the implementation of the Rural Development Programmes that are not available in the model. Nevertheless, this is the case at the level of detail that is modelled (essentially budgets and targeted sectors).

In general, when removing restrictions for obtaining the subsidies, such as production coupling for the VCS or greening restrictions, it is easier to spend all of the budget.

Table 2.A1.2. Hectares and herd sizes of groups of crops and animals (1000 heads or hectares)

Activity	Reference	CAP 2014-20	No-VCS	No-greening	Full flat rate
Utilized agricultural area	183 663	0.1%	0.1%	-0.4%	0.1%
Cereals	58 017	-2.0%	-1.8%	-0.4%	-2.1%
Oilseeds	13 444	-0.4%	-0.6%	0.6%	-0.4%
Other arable crops	6 108	7.4%	0.9%	8.2%	7.3%
- of which pulses	1 201	27.3%	1.6%	28.8%	27.1%
Vegetables and Permanent crops	14 022	0.0%	0.0%	0.0%	-0.1%
Fodder activities	83 316	0.6%	0.3%	-1.0%	0.5%
Set-aside and fallow land	8 756	5.7%	11.6%	-3.0%	5.5%
All ruminants	69 903	0.7%	-0.6%	0.7%	0.7%
All cattle activities	59 477	0.0%	-1.3%	0.1%	0.0%
Beef meat activities	18 032	-0.1%	-2.7%	0.0%	-0.1%
All Dairy	41 445	0.1%	-0.6%	0.1%	0.1%
Other animals	49 358	0.8%	0.6%	0.9%	0.8%
Pasture	59 520	1.9%	1.9%	-1.3%	1.8%
Arable land	124 143	-0.8%	-0.7%	0.0%	-0.8%

Table 2.A1.3. Production (1 000 tons or index) of selected categories of commodities.

	Reference	CAP 2014-20	No-VCS	No-greening	Full flat rate
Cereals	321 356	-1.4%	-1.3%	-0.1%	-1.4%
Oilseeds	36 472	-0.4%	-0.5%	0.3%	-0.5%
Other arable field crops	176 071	1.7%	-0.8%	2.8%	1.7%
Vegetables and Permanent crops	139 601	0.0%	0.0%	0.0%	0.0%
Meat	46 301	0.0%	-0.1%	0.1%	-0.1%
- Beef	7 980	0.1%	-1.1%	0.2%	0.1%
- Pork meat	23 508	-0.1%	0.0%	0.0%	-0.1%
- Sheep and goat meat	1 060	5.8%	4.8%	5.9%	5.8%
- Poultry meat	13 753	-0.4%	-0.2%	-0.3%	-0.4%
Other Animal products	191 474	0.0%	-0.2%	0.1%	0.0%
- Raw milk	156 517	0.0%	0.0%	0.1%	0.0%
- Eggs	7 531	-0.3%	-0.1%	-0.1%	-0.3%

Table 2.A1.4. Producer prices of agricultural commodities (EUR/t)

	Reference	CAP 2014-20	No-VCS	No-greening	Full flat rate
Cereals	156	1.8%	1.3%	0.6%	1.9%
Oilseeds	341	1.4%	0.7%	0.5%	1.5%
Other arable field crops	79	-1.0%	0.6%	-2.3%	-0.9%
Vegetables and Permanent crops	695	0.2%	0.3%	-0.1%	0.2%
Meat	2 205	0.0%	0.5%	-0.3%	0.0%
- Beef	3 795	-0.1%	2.3%	-0.3%	-0.1%
- Pork meat	1 907	0.1%	0.1%	-0.1%	0.1%
- Sheep and goat meat	5 703	-6.4%	-5.3%	-6.5%	-6.4%
- Poultry meat	1 521	0.3%	0.3%	0.1%	0.4%
Other Animal products	436	-0.1%	0.1%	-0.3%	-0.1%
- Raw milk	394	-0.1%	0.0%	-0.3%	-0.1%
- Eggs	1 280	0.5%	0.3%	0.2%	0.5%

Table 2.A1.5. Agricultural income for cereals by member state under CAP 2014-20 (million euro/year)

	Reference			CAP 2014-20		[Δ to ref]
	Market income	Direct payments	Total income	Market income	Direct payments	Total income
European Union 28	4 777	16 039	20 815	962	-1 369	-407
European Union 15	3 504	11 691	15 194	646	-1 196	-551
European Union 13	1 430	4 348	5 778	311	-172	138
Belgium	-157	160	2	24	-44	-20
Denmark	-509	530	22	53	-66	-13
Germany	1 152	2 420	3 572	144	-210	-66
Austria	-45	403	358	14	-47	-33
Netherlands	-88	92	4	10	-12	-2
France	828	2 350	3 179	207	-272	-65
Portugal	-11	34	24	2	11	14
Spain	1 223	1 281	2 504	68	-3	65
Greece	269	409	679	0	-110	-109
Italy	619	1 495	2 114	43	-196	-153
Ireland	22	77	98	4	-14	-10
Finland	-374	921	546	-4	-4	-8
Sweden	-194	272	78	12	-38	-26
United Kingdom	448	1 247	1 695	65	-192	-127
Czech Republic	127	471	598	20	-57	-37
Estonia	11	48	59	3	23	26
Hungary	-99	633	534	52	-76	-24
Lithuania	38	162	200	18	33	52
Latvia	-13	65	53	3	45	48
Poland	313	1 734	2 047	101	-146	-45
Slovenia	9	56	65	2	-15	-13
Slovak Republic	-45	160	115	9	2	12
Croatia	150	15	165	13	80	93
Cyprus	-2	27	24	0	-3	-3
Malta	-1	3	2	0	-1	-1
Bulgaria	111	313	424	22	-51	-29
Romania	911	662	1 573	59	-9	51

Table 2.A1.6. Agricultural income for ruminants by member state under CAP 2014-20 (million euro/year)

	Reference			CAP 2014-20		[Δ to ref]
	Market income	Direct payments	Total income	Market income	Direct payments	Total income
European Union 28	25 665	4 475	30 141	-1 307	2 714	1 407
European Union 15	27 334	4 153	31 487	-702	1 646	944
European Union 13	-1 232	322	-910	-585	1 068	482
Belgium	976	41	1 017	-30	97	67
Denmark	704	54	758	-12	46	34
Germany	4 303	333	4 636	-104	106	2
Austria	1 042	348	1 390	21	-40	-20
Netherlands	3 102	4	3 106	-2	6	4
France	4 383	793	5 176	-237	549	312
Portugal	813	93	906	-8	15	7
Spain	2 445	655	3 100	56	-91	-35
Greece	-6	76	70	20	39	59
Italy	1 221	266	1 487	-109	211	102
Ireland	2 540	447	2 987	-15	63	48
Finland	386	562	948	-65	64	-2
Sweden	-779	30	-749	46	91	137
United Kingdom	6 052	452	6 503	-250	491	241
Czech Republic	-96	65	-31	-41	60	19
Estonia	41	17	58	-14	28	14
Hungary	44	48	92	-45	112	67
Lithuania	301	27	328	-42	106	65
Latvia	62	17	79	-26	49	23
Poland	1 254	49	1 303	-133	274	142
Slovenia	7	29	36	-4	10	6
Slovak Republic	169	21	191	-10	41	30
Croatia	-326	0	-326	-26	30	5
Cyprus	-32	8	-24	-4	6	2
Malta	-22	1	-22	-1	2	0
Bulgaria	-33	18	-15	-34	82	49
Romania	-2 896	22	-2 874	-217	267	50

Table 2.A1.7. Tax payer expenditures for the CAP and national co-financing or state aid (million euro/year)

	Reference	CAP 2014-20	No-VCS	No-greening	Full flat rate
European Union 28	55 630	-720	-396	-575	-716
Belgium	687	-48	-47	-50	-48
Denmark	1 092	-67	-67	-69	-67
Germany	6 408	-216	-217	-222	-216
Austria	1 732	-9	-9	-8	-9
Netherlands	841	-97	-97	-97	-97
France	8 299	-286	-263	-297	-286
Portugal	551	48	49	48	48
Spain	5 898	-77	-44	-72	-77
Greece	2 446	-591	-550	-588	-586
Italy	5 608	-327	-296	-326	-328
Ireland	2 073	-45	-41	-46	-45
Finland	2 357	-127	-116	-128	-127
Sweden	1 338	-244	-241	-248	-244
United Kingdom	5 477	-19	-18	140	-19
Czech Republic	1 278	-25	0	-26	-25
Estonia	150	84	84	84	84
Hungary	1 314	65	93	67	65
Lithuania	559	187	194	186	187
Latvia	239	174	176	174	174
Poland	3 767	219	274	222	219
Slovenia	223	-9	-7	-9	-9
Slovak Republic	523	50	63	51	50
Croatia	40	258	260	257	258
Cyprus	88	-5	-5	-5	-5
Malta	10	-1	0	-1	-1
Bulgaria	871	30	65	30	30
Romania	1 763	357	366	359	357

Annex 2.A2

Implementation of voluntary coupled support by member states

Table 2.A2.1. Decisions taken by member states – Voluntary Coupled Support by sector in 2015
(EUR million)

	AT	BE	BG	CY	CZ	DK	DE	EE	EL	ES	FI	FR	HR	HU	IE	IT	LT	LU	LV	MT	NL	PL	PT	RO	SE	SI	SK	UK	EU-28	Share of total VCS
Cereals	-	-	-	-	-	-	-	-	9	-	2	7	-	-	-	60	-	-	3	-	-	-	-	-	-	7	-	-	87	2%
Rice	-	-	-	-	-	-	-	-	8	12	-	-	-	2	-	23	-	-	-	-	-	-	6	6	-	-	-	-	57	1%
Oilseeds	-	-	-	-	-	-	-	-	-	-	-	-	-	-	-	-	-	-	1	-	-	-	-	-	-	-	-	-	1	0%
Olive oil	-	-	-	-	-	-	-	-	-	-	-	-	-	-	-	70	-	-	-	-	-	-	-	-	-	-	-	-	70	2%
Nuts	-	-	-	-	-	-	-	-	-	14	-	-	-	-	-	-	-	-	-	-	-	-	-	-	-	-	-	-	14	0%
Sugar beet	-	-	-	-	17	-	-	-	5	17	1	-	3	8	-	17	-	-	0.2	-	-	81	-	18	-	-	8	-	174	4%
Beef and veal	12	83	27	-	24	24	-	1	29	228	56	652	8	40	-	108	17	-	3	0.5	2	172	60	11	91	4	8	45	1 706	42%
Milk and milk products	-	3	24	3	50	-	-	2	-	94	32	135	9	69	-	89	24	-	12	2	-	152	13	78	-	5	33	-	829	20%
Sheepmeat and goatmeat	0.9	0.7	11	0.7	3	-	-	0.4	33	169	3	135	2	22	-	15	2	-	0.3	0.1	1	5	36	25	-	-	6	8	478	12%
Silkworms	-	-	-	-	-	-	-	-	1	-	-	-	-	-	-	-	-	-	-	-	-	-	-	0.0	-	-	-	-	0.8	0%
Seeds	-	-	-	-	-	-	-	-	3	-	-	0.5	-	-	-	-	-	-	1	-	-	-	-	0.8	-	-	-	-	5	0%
Fruit and vegetables	-	-	41	0.3	9	-	-	1	16	6	1	15	2	34	-	11	5	-	2	1	-	19	3	32	-	2	2	-	203	5%
Hops	-	-	-	-	3	-	-	-	-	-	-	0	-	-	-	-	-	-	-	-	-	0.8	-	0.1	-	-	0.1	-	5	0%
Protein crops	-	-	16	-	17	-	-	-	7	45	6	142	4	27	3	24	14	0.2	4	-	-	68	-	49	-	3	-	-	428	10%
Grain legumes	-	-	-	-	-	-	-	-	5	1	-	-	-	-	-	12	-	-	-	-	-	-	-	0.4	-	-	-	-	18	0%
Starch potato	-	-	-	-	3	-	-	-	-	-	4	2	-	-	-	-	-	-	-	-	-	9	-	-	-	-	-	-	17	0%
Hemp	-	-	-	-	-	-	-	-	-	-	-	2	-	-	-	-	-	-	-	-	-	0.1	-	0.2	-	-	-	-	2	0%
Flax	-	-	-	-	-	-	-	-	-	-	-	-	-	-	-	-	-	-	-	-	-	1	-	-	-	-	-	-	0.6	0%
Total	13	87	119	4	127	24	-	4	116	585	105	1 091	28	201	3	429	63	0.2	27	3	4	507	118	219	91	21	57	53	4 097	100%

Note: Regional measures are attributed to the relevant sector at member state level. –: no VCS is provided. Germany is represented for completeness, it does not attribute VCS. One decimal point is shown for amounts smaller than EUR 1 million.

Source: Voluntary Coupled Support, Decisions notified to the Commission by 1 August 2014. Informative note DG Agriculture and Rural Development European Commission 29 July 2015 and Voluntary coupled support - Other sectors supported, notifications of decisions taken by member states by 1 August 2014, informative note December 2015. Member state totals are calculated.

Chapter 3

Risk management

Risk management tools aim to address downward income fluctuations. Income risks stemming from weather fluctuations, natural disasters, pests and diseases have always been important in the agricultural sector. In a context of more open agricultural markets, farm revenues are now more directly influenced by price developments than a decade ago, reinforcing the need for a comprehensive risk assessment. The CAP contains several measures that are labelled specifically as risk management instruments, but many more measures and payments directly or indirectly influence the risk exposure of farmers. This chapter reviews these measures and builds on previous work on risk management to describe selected examples of risk management strategies in Spain, the Netherlands, Canada and the United States.

This section offers a succinct review of risk management measures in the CAP 2014-20 and discusses those measures that affect risk exposure and influence the uptake of risk management tools by farmers. While it does not replace a risk management review, it uses the considerable volume of work done over the years by the OECD on managing risk in agriculture to illustrate, categorise and assess how the CAP enables farmers to anticipate and cope with risk (OECD, 2009, 2011).

When discussing risk management instruments under the CAP, due consideration should be given to the budgetary context in which it is developed. The financial rules set by the European Union's budgetary framework; the Multiannual Financial Framework (MFF), ensure control on all EU budgets, including the CAP. The MFF fixes the overall annual ceiling on CAP expenditure. While unspent monies are to be reverted to the direct payments budget, excess spending is not permitted and makes it necessary to control and plan the budget annually. In a context where overall amounts are fixed, exceptional spending can only occur if funds are redirected from other spending. The pace of decision making and the current structure of the CAP; where 77% of the budget is locked into direct payments to farmers (Chapter 2), leave little room for ad hoc and exceptional measures. It is all the more important that farmers engage in developing their own risk management approaches. Moreover, direct payments offered to all farmers accounted for approximately 14% of gross farm receipts during the 2013-15 period on average, as measured by the OECD indicators of support. Such payments provide a stable and predictable support base and limit farm receipt variability. As such, they reduce incentives for some to engage in risk management.

3.1.   Risk management in the CAP

Increasing attention has recently been given to risk management tools and their use by farmers in the European Union to address downward fluctuations in income. Income risks stemming from weather fluctuations, natural disasters, pests and diseases have always been important in the agricultural sector. With much reduced emphasis on market measures and more openness of the EU agricultural markets, farm revenues are now more directly influenced by price developments than a decade ago, reinforcing the need for a comprehensive risk assessment. The CAP contains several measures that are labelled specifically as risk management instruments, but many more measures and payments directly or indirectly influence the risk exposure of farmers and should hence be included in a holistic assessment of risk management instruments.

This chapter builds on the OECD risk management framework (OECD, 2011) and on reviews of EU member states' risk management strategies (Antón and Kimura, 2011; Melyukhina, 2011) as well as recent experiences in Canada (OECD, 2011) and the United States (Box 3.1).

Box 3.1. Agricultural risk management: A holistic approach

The agricultural sector has always been exposed to price volatility – indeed, swings in product and input prices tend to be larger in agriculture than in other sectors. This is partly due to the reliance of production on natural conditions and weather influences, and partly to the specificities of agricultural commodity markets that can lead to sharp reactions by prices to changes in supply. In general, price spikes are more likely than troughs, as many agricultural products can be stored when prices are low and sold later.

Disease outbreaks and adverse weather events, such as floods and droughts, also contribute to supply volatility and can negatively impact producer incomes, markets, trade and consumers. These are expected to become more frequent as a result of climate change.

Risks in agriculture are interconnected, sometimes compounding and sometimes *offsetting* each other. If the prices of inputs (such as fertiliser) and outputs (such as agricultural commodities) move in the same direction, for example, the impact on net returns is reduced. Production risks can be partially offset by price movements: when crop yields are low but prices are high, revenues are more stable. It is the net risk effect on income that matters.

OECD analysis of risk management in agriculture has identified three layers of risks which require different responses:

- *Normal* variations in production, prices and weather do not require any specific policy response. These can be directly managed by farmers as part of normal business strategy, via the diversification of production or the use of production technologies which make yields less variable. Income-smoothing through tax instruments for businesses is also part of normal risk management.

- At the other extreme, infrequent but *catastrophic* events that affect many or all farmers over a wide area will usually be beyond farmers' or markets' capacity to cope. A severe and widespread drought is one example. The outbreak and spread of a highly contagious and damaging disease is another. Governments may need to intervene in such cases.

- In between the normal and the catastrophic risk layers lies a *marketable* risk layer that can be handled through market tools, such as insurance and futures markets, or through co-operative arrangements between farmers. Examples of marketable risks include hail damage and some variations in market prices.

Risk management tools are essential to enable farmers to anticipate, avoid and react to shocks. A broad approach is needed that recognises how different sources of risk, different strategies and different actors – both public and private – interact. Governments should adopt a holistic approach to risk management, assessing all risks and their relationships to each other, and avoiding focusing on a single source of risk, such as prices. Increased co-operation and communication with stakeholders – farmers and veterinarians included – is essential for better policy design in order to understand the capacity of farmers to manage risk and the additional sources needed to improve responses. Governments can also play a primary role in facilitating good "start-up" conditions, by providing information, regulation and training for the development of market-based risk management tools such as futures, insurance and marketing contracts. The OECD has developed three guiding principles of good design of risk management policies in agriculture:

- Agricultural risk management policies should focus on catastrophic risks that are rare but cause significant damage to many farmers at the same time. The procedures, responsibilities and limits of the policy response – including explicit triggering criteria and types and levels of assistance – should be defined in advance of the event.

- Policies should not provide support for the management of "normal" risk. This should be the preserve of farmers themselves. Minimum intervention prices or payments that are triggered when prices or returns are low may actually be counter-productive, as they tend to induce more risky farming practices.

Policies should also avoid crowding out the development of private insurance markets by subsidised insurance. Subsidising insurance can be costly for governments and has not deterred pressure for additional ad hoc governmental assistance after a catastrophic event.

Source: Reproduced from *Agricultural Policy Monitoring and Evaluation 2016*, OECD (2016a).

Risk management instruments

Measures branded as risk management belong to Priority 3 of pillar 2 under the title **Farm risk prevention and management,**[1] and are co-financed by member states (Cordier, 2014). They are organised along two dimensions: a) insurance premium subsidies; and b) support to mutual funds. Twelve member states have included this pillar 2 measure in their RDP with an allocated overall budget close to EUR 3 billion (Table 3.1). Member states' take up of the measure represents 2% of their total rural development expenditure, on average; it is generally less than 4% with the exception of Italy where it approximates 8%.

Table 3.1. **Member states take up of risk management instruments over 2014-20**

	Risk management instruments (RM) (million EUR)	Total rural development expenditure (TRD) (million EUR)	Share of RM in TRD
Belgium	5	1 579	0%
Croatia	57	2 383	2%
France	601	16 985	4%
Hungary	95	4 174	2%
Italy	1 591	20 925	8%
Latvia	10	1 532	1%
Lithuania	17	1 978	1%
Malta	3	130	2%
Netherlands	54	1 645	3%
Portugal	53	4 721	1%
Romania	200	9 473	2%
Spain	14	13 155	0%
EU28	2 700	158 627	2%

Source: OECD calculation based on national 2014-20 RDP budget as published in: http://ec.europa.eu/agriculture/rural-development-2014-2020/country-files/index_en.htm, 2016.

The first dimension encourages farm participation in insurance schemes. It offers farmers an incentive to take up crop, animal and plant **insurance schemes** against economic losses caused by adverse climatic events, animal or plant diseases, pest infestation, or an environmental incident. Support covers up to 65% of the insurance premium, typically within the marketable risk layer of the OECD risk management framework.

This measure may compete with, or add support to, existing and well-functioning insurance systems in member states. For example, in Spain agricultural insurance has a long history and was identified as the main risk management instrument in the crop sector (Antón and Kimura, 2011). Public-Private insurance schemes are in place (Figure 3.1) and CAP support is limited to small amounts in one region (Table 3.1).

The second and third dimensions of the measure support up to 65% of eligible costs covered by mutual funds. These funds are subsidised for compensating economic losses resulting from events outside the farmer's control, such as adverse climatic or environmental events or animal or plant disease. They are also subsidised for compensating a severe drop in farm income. While the constitution of mutual funds is open to several actors, in practice, their use to cover production loss has generally been implemented through agricultural cooperatives. This measure may be used to offer them indirect support. Alternatively, the measure can also incentivise other intermediaries to offer mutual fund services to the agricultural sector.

Figure 3.1. Risk management strategies and policies in Spain

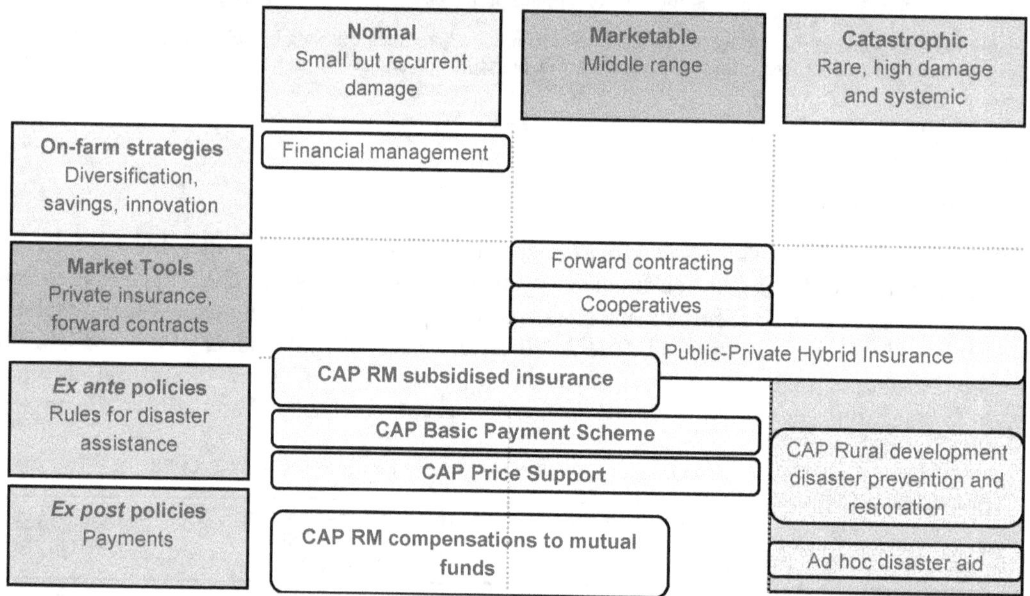

Source: Adapted from Antón, J. and S. Kimura (2011), "Risk Management in Agriculture in Spain", *OECD Food, Agriculture and Fisheries Papers*, No. 43, OECD Publishing, Paris, http://dx.doi.org/10.1787/5kgj0d57w0wd-en.

When considering the RDP **Farm risk prevention and management** title in general, one realises that a larger group of member states is involved. Overall, 21 member states have embraced a host of available instruments to address farm risk and use measures going beyond the insurance premium subsidy and support to mutual funds that are explicitly identified in pillar 2 as risk management instruments (Table 3.2). As explained in Box 2.2 of Chapter 2, within a defined priority, twenty measures are available that member states may mobilise. The choice of measure determines the implementation mode. Table 3.2 illustrates the measures implemented by member states to serve priority "Farm risk prevention and management". For example, "Knowledge transfer and information actions", "Investment in physical assets", and "Advisory services, farm management and farm relief services"[2] are the three measures that Ireland implements under this priority. Germany has used "Disaster prevention and relief" and "Advisory services, farm management and farm relief services" to serve the same priority.[3] Similarly, the Netherlands has chosen to serve "Farm risk prevention and management" by supporting "Risk management" measures, i.e. insurance subsidies and support to mutual funds, described above.

Table 3.2. Member states choice instruments under Farm risk prevention and management
(EUR million unless otherwise indicated)

	Knowledge	Advisory services	Investments	Disaster prevention and restoration	Forest investments	Cooperation	Risk management	Total Rural Development expenditure (TRD)	Share of Farm risk prevention in Total Rural Development
Austria	1	0				0		7 812	0%
Belgium							5	1 579	0%
Bulgaria	0	0						2 918	0%
Croatia				118			57	2 383	7%
Estonia		0						993	0%
France	5	2		12		5	601	16 985	4%
Germany	0	26		1 201				16 886	7%
Greece				52				5 880	1%
Hungary				21			95	4 174	3%
Ireland	25	6	25					3 916	1%
Italy	6	8		229	25	8	1 591	20 925	9%
Latvia				5			10	1 532	1%
Lithuania							17	1 978	1%
Malta							3	130	2%
Netherlands							54	1 645	3%
Poland	3			415				13 513	3%
Portugal		1		24			53	4 721	2%
Romania	3						200	9 473	2%
Slovakia	1	0		70				2 080	3%
Spain	1	1		20		3	14	13 155	0%
United Kingdom	2	3				8		7 626	0%
EU28	47	48	25	2 168	25	24	2 700	158 627	3%
Share in Total	0%	0%	0%	1%	0%	0%	2%		

Note: Numbers reported above correspond to member state national RDP programmes under sub-priority 2: Risk management in agriculture of Priority 3: Promoting food chain organisation, including processing and marketing of agricultural products, animal welfare and risk management in agriculture. Empty cells indicate that no expenditure has occurred while the value 0 corresponds to the rounded value of expenditure that has occurred.

Source: OECD calculation based on national 2014-20 RDP budget as published in: http://ec.europa.eu/agriculture/rural-development-2014-2020/country-files/index_en.htm, 2016.

Besides risk management measures, the most common instruments implemented by member states support investments for "Disaster prevention and restoration" and capacity building with "Knowledge transfer" and "Advisory services". Investments for "Disaster prevention and restoration" attract the largest budget, a little more than EUR 2 billion, and cover up to 80% of eligible investment costs for prevention operations carried out by individual farmers, the percentage is raised to 100% if the investment is carried out by farmer groups. Also fully covered is the eligible investment cost of operations to restore agricultural land and production potential damaged by natural disasters and catastrophic events. The programme specifically excludes compensation of income loss. By offering a higher support rate to investments by producer groups, the programme also strengthens the impact of measures supporting the formation of producer groups.

Previous work on risk management has described and evaluated agricultural insurance schemes and found that they are widespread (OECD, 2009, 2011). The main advantages of such programmes consist in farmer participation, transparency of the schemes and that they generally allow governments to pass on implementation to the private sector. Market-based privately operated schemes are typically available for specific risks, but multi-risk insurance schemes are generally subsidised, and sometimes government operated. In the European Union, such subsidies are CAP co-funded and member states have had different strategies in adopting them as illustrated in Figures 3.1 and 3.2. Support to insurance systems may also be part of national strategies and funded from national budgets of member states. As such EU state aid rules apply (Box 3.2).

Another illustration can be found in the US 2014 Farm Bill that offers farmers a menu of subsidised risk management options as described in Box 3.6.

Figure 3.2. Risk management strategies and policies in the Netherlands

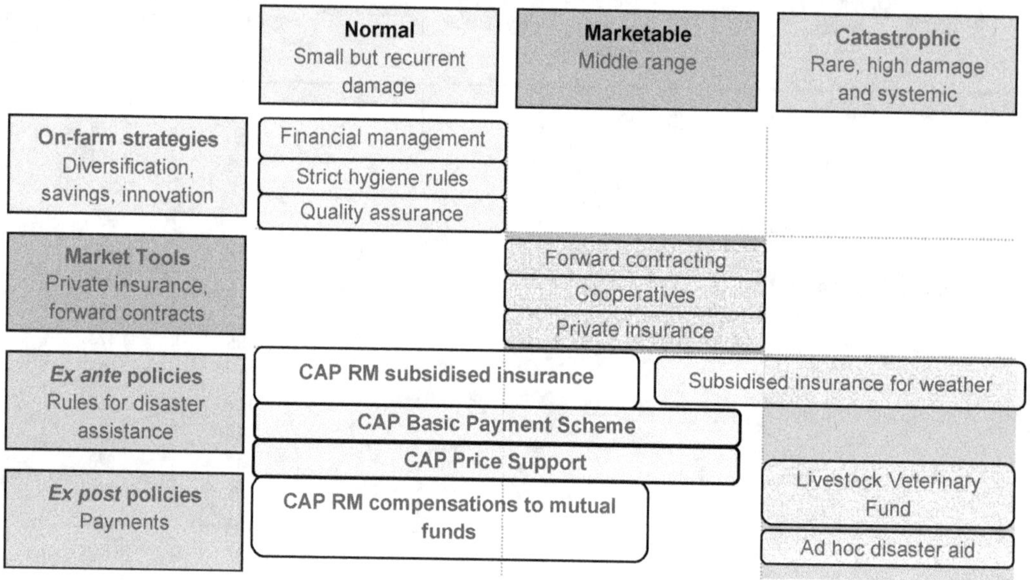

Source: Adapted from Melyukhina, O. (2011), "Risk Management in Agriculture in The Netherlands", *OECD Food, Agriculture and Fisheries Papers*, No. 41, OECD Publishing, Paris, http://dx.doi.org/10.1787/5kgj0d5lqn48-en.

Other options exist that address income variability through savings accounts and by smoothing farm income variations. Such a system is available in Australia where the Farm Management Deposits scheme waives income tax on amounts that stay on deposit for at least 12 months. Under special circumstances, the funds can be used while benefits are maintained despite a shorter period (Keogh et al., 2011). In Canada, the AgriInvest saving account offers farmers a government-financed match to their deposits. The account can be used to overcome income drops and to fund on-farm investments mitigating risks or improving market income (Box 3.5).

Alternatively, multi-year income tax averaging schemes allow taxable income to be spread over several years, thereby reducing variability of disposable income. Such measures are in use in some EU member states (OECD, 2009). In the Netherlands these are not specific to agriculture. Income tax averaging is also implemented in Ireland. However, as part of the 2017 Budget, the "Income Averaging" system has been adjusted to allow farmers to opt-out in exceptional years (Government of Ireland, 2016).

Box 3.2. Provisions for crisis management under EU state aid legislation

EU state aid legislation in agriculture provides, amongst other measures for the following risk and crisis management measures:

- Aid to make good the damage caused by natural disasters or exceptional occurrences.
- Aid to compensate for damage caused by adverse climatic events which can be assimilated to a natural disaster.
- Aid for the costs of the prevention, control and eradication of animal diseases and plant pests and aid to make good the damage caused by animal diseases and plant pests.
- Aid for fallen stock.
- Aid to compensate for the damage caused by protected animals.
- Aid for the payment of insurance premiums.
- Aid for financial contributions to mutual funds.
- Aid for Closing Production Capacity.

The aid for insurance premiums is provided for in both the CAP guidelines and in Regulation No 702/2014. The difference between the notified aid and the block-exempted aid lays within the scope of the beneficiaries. Block-exempted aid is open to small and medium sized enterprises, while notified aid is open also to large enterprises though large enterprises have to prove the need for aid by presenting counterfactual scenario.

The substantial conditions for granting such aid are summarised as follows:

- The aid is open to undertakings active in the primary agricultural production.
- The aid must not constitute a barrier to the operation of the internal market for insurance services.
- The eligible costs are the costs of insurance premiums covering the damage caused by natural disasters or exceptional occurrences, adverse climatic events which can be assimilated to a natural disaster, animal diseases and plant pests, the removal and destruction of fallen stock and damage caused by protected animals, as well as by other adverse climatic events and/or damage caused by environmental incidents.
- The gross aid intensity must not exceed 65% of the cost of the insurance premium, with the exception of aid for the removal and destruction of fallen stock, where the aid intensity must not exceed 100% of the cost of the insurance premium as regards insurance premiums for the removal of fallen stock and 75% of the cost of the insurance premium as regards insurance premiums for the destruction of such fallen stock.

Sources:
General information on EU State Aid: http://ec.europa.eu/competition/state_aid/scoreboard/index_en.html
Compilation of EU State Aid rules in force: http://ec.europa.eu/competition/state_aid/legislation/compilation/index_en.html
Competition cases database: http://ec.europa.eu/competition/elojade/isef/index.cfm?clear=1&policy_area_id=3
Statistics on state aid expenditures in the EU agricultural and forestry sectors and in rural areas:
http://ec.europa.eu/eurostat/tgm_comp/table.do?tab=table&init=1&plugin=1&language=en&pcode=comp_ag_01

Further information on state aid policy in agriculture, forestry and in rural areas: https://ec.europa.eu/agriculture/stateaid_en.

Other measures that affect risk exposure

From a farm management point of view, the impact of policies on farm receipts may determine farmer risk perception and willingness to reduce risk exposure. During the 2013-15 period, support to farmers, as measured by the percentage PSE, made up 18% of farm receipts on average (Table 3.3). This means that, on average, 18% of the farm revenues resulted from policies and provided a cushion against downward income fluctuations.

Most CAP instruments affect exposure to risk (Table 3.4). As described in greater length in Chapter 2, public intervention in markets has been maintained and support to private storage has been expanded to new sectors. In addition, in cases of so-called market disturbance or other exceptional situations, other instruments under the CMO could apply, including exceptional measures (Box 3.3), or the crisis reserve used. These can further reduce the incentives for farmers to develop their own risk management strategies. It is important to note that in recent years the relative size of the CMO in the CAP budget has been reduced and it now accounts for about 3% of the overall CAP public expenditure. The activation conditions and modalities for exceptional public assistance are yet to be defined. *Ex ante* provisions with regards to the circumstances under which the CMO or the crisis reserve are mobilised would improve farmers' foresight and enable them to take these measures into account when they develop their risk management strategy.

Table 3.3. Share of support in gross farm receipts (%PSE)

	2013-15*
Percentage PSE	18.2%
A. Support based on commodity outputs	4.4%
B. Payments based on input use	2.5%
C. Payments based on current A/An/R/I, production required	2.8%
D. Payments based on non-current A/An/R/I, production required	0.0%
E. Payments based on non-current A/An/R/I, production not required	7.9%
F. Payments based on non-commodity criteria	0.5%
G. Miscellaneous payments	0.1%

Note: The 2013-15 average does not take into account pillar 2 payments of the CAP 2014-20 as these were not implemented.

Source: OECD (2016b), "Producer and Consumer Support Estimates", OECD Agriculture Statistics (database), http://dx.doi.org/10.1787/agr-pcse-data-en.

Table 3.4. A holistic view of CAP risk-related expenditure in 2016

Estimated 2016 CAP expenditure (EUR)		Share in CAP EU budget	Share in CAP total public expenditure (sum of EU and national funding)
Interventions in agricultural markets (CMO)	2 703 000 000	4.4%	3.7%
Direct Payments, of which:	39 445 708 157	64.3%	54.5%
Decoupled direct payments, of which:	34 269 200 000	55.8%	47.4%
Greening	12 239 000 000	19.9%	16.9%
Coupled support	4 734 808 157	7.7%	6.5%
Crisis reserve	**441 600 000**	0.7%	0.6%
Rural Development EU funding	18 671 922 495	30.1%	25.6%
Rural Development national funding	*10 958 459 230*		15.0%
Rural Development total public expenditure, of which:	***29 630 381 725***		40.6%
Priority 1: knowledge	*allocated all through other priorities*		
Priority 2: competitiveness	*6 092 971 326*		8.4%
Priority 3: food chain organisations	*3 007 480 265*		4.1%
Priority 4: ecosystems	*13 205 806 539*		18.1%
Priority 5: resource efficiency	*2 214 009 101*		3.0%
Priority 6: social inclusion	*4 345 519 913*		6.0%
Policy Strategy	34 183 167	0.1%	0.0%
Horizon 2020	214 205 269	0.3%	0.3%
CAP EU funding	**61 380 834 429**		
CAP total public expenditure	**72 339 293 659**		

Notes: OECD calculations based on national Rural Development Programmes are italicised. Total public expenditure includes national co-financing and national top-ups .Totals in the RDP do not add up as Technical Assistance and Discontinued measures are not included.

Source: EU budget 2017 at http://eur-lex.europa.eu/budget/data/DB/2017/en/SEC03.pdf and OECD calculations based on national 2014-20 RDP budget as published in: http://ec.europa.eu/agriculture/rural-development-2014-2020/country-files/index_en.htm, 2016.

Box 3.3 offers a short description that illustrates how an array of exceptional measures has been developed and deployed since August 2014. The measures are expected to reduce farmer exposure to risk and enable the sector to transit through circumstances that have been qualified as "severe". While a number of measures have increased farm resilience through greater implication in own risk management, others may have confirmed reliance on policy intervention. In this respect, the recommendations of the Agricultural Markets Task Force emphasised the need for risk management tools and for better supply chain integration of farmers (Box 3.4).

Other elements of the CAP also impact farm exposure to risk and thus influence farmers risk management strategies and use of risk management instruments. The most prominent, from a public expenditure point of view, are the guaranteed **direct payments** to farmers under P1 as they account for 55% of the CAP public expenditure. Using the 2016 PSE calculations, direct payments made up the largest share of support, as they accounted for approximately 14% of gross farm receipts during the 2013-15 period. Such payments provide a stable and predictable support and limit farm receipt variability. A range of decoupled per hectare payments offer an income base to all agricultural holdings: the BPS and the SAPS,[4] and Greening payments. However, as these payments are disbursed per hectare of eligible land, their benefits are likely to be mostly captured by land-endowed holdings or crop sectors and benefit less the livestock sector.

Box 3.3. CAP 2014-20 responses to recent market developments

Within the EU legislative framework regarding measures against market disturbance, as defined in Article 219 of Regulation 1308/2013 (OJ, 2013b), a number of exceptional measures have been deployed since August 2014, when an import ban was imposed on EU dairy and fruit and vegetables by the Russian Federation. The ban was prolonged and its effects later coincided with other "severe market disturbance", as explained by the European Commission.

Some measures were tailored to the dairy sector. The public intervention for butter and SMP, that is typically open from 1 March to 30 September every year, was opened and prolonged to continuously apply from September 2014 till 30 September 2017 (OJ, 2014, 2015a, 2016a). The same extensions applied to private storage for butter and SMP. In the case of cheese, private storage was only opened temporarily in April 2014 and rapidly closed.

Further to, and reinforcing these measures, the public intervention ceilings for skimmed milk powder and butter were raised in 2016 from 109 000 tonnes and 60 000 tonnes respectively to 218 000 tonnes and 100 000 tonnes.

In 2014, direct support was offered to the dairy sectors in Baltic countries and Finland, EUR 28 million and EUR 11 million respectively, to be distributed to farmers to compensate their losses.

In 2016, the voluntary supply management (CMO article 222) was activated to enable producer organisations, interbranch organisations and cooperatives in the dairy sector to establish voluntary agreements on the planning of milk production for a period of six months. The scheme was endowed with EUR 150 million and member states were authorised to increase state aid to a maximum of EUR 15 000 per farmer per year, with no national ceiling (EC, 2016). A derogation to competition aid was also agreed without any costs involved.

A package was announced in October 2015 opening a EUR 420 million support budget to the livestock sectors. The budget was to be used to protect livestock farmers experiencing cash flow and treasury difficulties from the effects of market disturbances and member states could top up to par with state aid (OJ, 2015b).

In 2016 and payable from 2017 budgets, EUR 350 million was targeted to dairy and livestock producers to implement measures such as small scale farming, extensive production, environmental and climate friendly production, cooperation between farmers, improvement of quality and added value, training in financial instruments and risk management tools. In addition, member states can match with national funds.

Further to these, adjustments are proposed to the payment of the Voluntary Coupled Support to dairy cow herd owners, as a lump sum rather than per head of animal (OJ, 2016b).

As regards Fruit and vegetables, support measures are available for withdrawals of produce for free distribution and other purposes such as animal feed, composting, distillation, as well as "non-harvesting" and "green harvesting".

Sources: EC (2016), OJ (2014), OJ (2015a), OJ (2015b), OJ (2016a), OJ (2016b).

Over time, a greater share of payments has become conditional on compulsory farming practices, first with the Good Agricultural and Environmental Conditions of cross-compliance, and now, with the greening payment of the CAP 2014-20. The greening conditions, where they apply, may impose changes in farm management that narrow the production choices and restrain business management strategy options as a means to mitigate risks. Alternatively, environmental outcomes could have been identified for farmers to achieve, while leaving it to them to decide on the means to achieve these targets. The difficulty of measuring environmental outcomes at farm level should not be underestimated, but improved technology, especially digitally enabled measuring and sensoring, may offer viable solutions in the future.

In addition to decoupled direct payments, member states may grant **sector specific payments**. For example, all EU member states, except Germany, have attributed part of their direct payment budget to support selected agricultural sectors under the Voluntary Coupled Support scheme (Chapter 2). The scheme, which is open to all farmers in eligible sectors, is based on area or headage and is unconditional on income. Other delivery means could be developed that are not linked to farmers' production and provide more incentive to diversify management and production choices, possible options were considered by the Agricultural Market Task Force (AMTF) (Box 3.4).

The CAP also funds measures deemed to improve farmer participation in supply chains and competitiveness. As such, the support provided to set up **producer groups** and stimulus for cooperation is also put forward as means to improve access to markets and increase market income predictability. In its recommendations, the AMTF that was launched in 2016, identified areas for improvement (Box 3.4).

Box 3.4. The Agricultural Markets Task Force

In January 2016, the European Commission launched a high-level advisory group, the "Agricultural Markets Task Force (AMTF)". The AMTF was tasked to provide advice and expertise concerning the functioning of the supply chain and the position of farmers therein, and to make recommendations, taking into account global challenges for sustainable agriculture.

The AMTF report, published in November 2016, made concrete recommendations in main policy areas:

- **Market transparency**, making price reporting along the chain obligatory; improving the existing market observatories; and publishing "Food euro" calculations for major food products.

- **Risk management**, making the current EU toolkit of instruments more attractive and coherent with member state instruments; looking into the possibility of EU co-financing of reinsurance schemes; and setting up an EU platform, including member states and stakeholders, to allow the exchange of best practices concerning agricultural risk management.

- **Futures markets**, prioritising awareness-raising and training measures for farmers and farmer organisations; and enabling through market transparency measures reliable and credible price references which are necessary for futures markets to develop.

- **Use of contracts** (contractualisation), making a written contract obligatory if requested by the farmer; and enabling *ex ante* value-sharing mechanisms through collective negotiations between operators in the food chain.

- **Unfair Trading Practices**, introducing EU framework legislation; strengthening enforcement regimes in member states; and progressing with the work of the High-Level Forum on the Better Functioning of the Food Supply Chain[5] and the voluntary industry-led Supply Chain Initiative.[6]

- **Producer cooperation** (competition law), making the rules clearer and more workable for farmers; clearly exempting joint planning and joint negotiating from competition law, if carried out by a recognised producer organisation.

- **Access to finance**, encouraging the roll-out of pilot projects by the European Investment Bank (EIB) for the agriculture sector; developing targeted financial instruments by leveraging CAP money to pull in private funds; and exploring the possibility of setting-up of an export credit guarantee facility at the EIB for agricultural exports to new or risky markets.

The AMTF also made some "general considerations concerning the CAP after 2020". The report stated that the "greater market-orientation of the Common Agricultural Policy (CAP)" and the trend towards "integration of European agriculture in global markets" should not be reversed. However, concern was expressed that farmers have become the main "shock absorber" in the supply chain, as regards market instability, such as price volatility or prolonged periods of low prices.

While acknowledging that, in the 2014 CAP reform, direct payment adjustments and a reinforced regulatory for farmer organisations had brought a welcome emphasis to producer organisations, their associations and inter-branch organisations, work was considered to be still "in progress". With regard to the current uncertainties in EU agriculture, climate change was picked out as "one of the most ominous of all global governance issues" and the value of assistance in the efforts for a transition of the EU farming sector at member state level was underlined.

The report also advocated a "rethink" of the direct payments policy and "a resource shift towards an integrated risk management policy at EU level that is complementary to existing strategies at member states level".

While sustainability considerations are expected to "continue to play a prominent role" and it was thought that the current emphasis on innovation needs to be "stepped up" and that the "centres for education and training in Europe have to be revitalised".

Source: European Commission, Agricultural Markets Task Force webpage at https://ec.europa.eu/agriculture/agri-markets-task-force_en.

The beneficial role that **knowledge and advisory services** can play in enabling farmers to develop profitable business strategies has also been highlighted in previous studies. Knowledge transfer and advisory services are frequently offered by member states as they may be mobilised to serve many aspects of farm management. As such, they reinforce farmer capacity to improve farm management techniques and alleviate risk. While the use of these measures is prevalent across all rural development priorities, their specific application to the Risk management priority is more limited (Table 3.5). Among the 13 member states who have taken it up, only Ireland attributes nearly 25% of its knowledge transfers and advisory services budget to risk management, most of the remaining 12 member states spend less than 2% of their knowledge and advisory budgets on risk management measures.

The use of knowledge and advisory services to encourage farmer take-up of risk management instruments was part of the recent package of measures deployed in 2016 to address so-called exceptional circumstances. The package included support to advisory services specifically to engage in risk management instruments (Box 3.3). However, the mix of measures on offer included a number of direct relief measures with monetary compensations associated. These measures are more likely to attract attention and, as a result, advisory services to help farmers' access to risk management instruments may have gone unnoticed.

Table 3.5. Share of knowledge transfer and advisory services in RDPs (EUR million)

	Knowledge transfer	Advisory Services	Total Public Expenditure	Share of knowledge transfer and advisory services in Total Public Expenditure	Share of risk management knowledge transfer and advisory services in total K&A
Austria	116	22	7 812	2%	1%
Belgium	38	21	1 579	4%	
Bulgaria	25	20	2 918	2%	1%
Croatia	13	21	2 383	1%	
Cyprus	2		243	1%	
Czech Republic	3	4	3 074	0%	
Denmark	37		907	4%	
Estonia	12	9	993	2%	0%
Finland	80	34	8 325	1%	
France	171	131	16 985	2%	3%
Germany	139	596	16 886	4%	4%
Greece	78	162	5 880	4%	
Hungary	54	45	4 174	2%	
Ireland	126	8	3 916	3%	23%
Italy	247	333	20 925	3%	2%
Latvia	33	10	1 532	3%	
Lithuania	23	5	1 978	1%	
Luxembourg			368	0%	
Malta	6	3	130	6%	
Netherlands	35	30	1 645	4%	
Poland	58	75	13 513	1%	2%
Portugal	31	34	4 721	1%	2%
Romania	67	71	9 473	1%	2%
Slovakia	14	4	2 080	1%	3%
Slovenia	13	11	1 107	2%	
Spain	148	219	13 155	3%	0%
Sweden	129	86	4 300	5%	
United Kingdom	170	87	7 626	3%	2%
EU28	1 868	2 041	158 627	2%	2%

Source: OECD calculations based on national 2014-20 RDP budget as published in: http://ec.europa.eu/agriculture/rural-development-2014-2020/country-files/index_en.htm, 2016.

Box 3.5. Agricultural risk management in Canada

Business Risk Management (BRM) instruments to support risk management in agriculture were implemented in 2013 as part of Growing Forward 2, the 5-year (2013-18) policy framework for Canadian agriculture and agri-food industry (GF2 website). BRM is a joint Federal and Provincial-Territorial agriculture programme (Figure 3.3). It covers a period of 5 years and contains 5 sub-programmes: AgriRisk, AgriInvest, AgriInsurance, AgriRecovery and AgriStability.

To increase producers' capability to address risks, **AgriRisk** provides financial and technical assistance to private sector and industry-led projects to research, develop, implement and deliver new tools to cope with risks in agriculture. Research and development projects are federally funded whereas implementation and delivery projects are cost shared with provinces or territories. **AgriInvest** is a producer-government saving-account system to be used in case of small income shortfalls or as a support for farm investments to mitigate risks or improving market income. Producers' annual deposits are based on a percentage of their allowable net sales and cannot exceed 100% of its allowable net sales. Farmers' deposits are matched up to 1% of their allowable net sales by federal and provincial-territorial governments and cannot exceed CAD 15 000 annually. Producers are given greater responsibility (than governments) for small losses while governments' assistance is focused on disasters.

AgriInsurance provides protection against production losses due to unforeseen events beyond a producer control. The programme is actuarially sound and coverage includes traditional field crops, horticultural crops, forage and pasture, but commodities eligible for coverage vary based on the provincial needs. Although the programme is crop-focused, livestock is eligible for AgriInsurance. Demand for production insurance plans related to the sector has been limited. Federal coverage is adjusted depending on loss-type from 20% for high-cost production loss to 36% for comprehensive production loss (all losses but catastrophic, high-cost and wildlife) and up-to 60% for catastrophic production loss and for wildlife compensation.

The disaster assistance programme, **AgriRecovery**, covers activities necessary to resume business operations or the cost of short-term actions necessary to reduce the impacts, where these costs are significant and beyond the producer's capacity to manage. Assistance to producers is given when Federal, Provincial and private mechanisms are not sufficient to recover. Government cost-sharing arrangement is assessed on a case-by-case basis in case of national disaster.

AgriStability is a margin-based instrument triggered when margins fall below 70% of the reference margin. The programme provides support for severe declines in income related to price and production issues and is available across all sectors. AgriStability expenditure is assessed and revised year by year based on the sector conditions. Payments are shared by federal and provincial governments at a 60-40 split. In 2014-15, little income stabilisation was needed. Although payouts were lower, administrative costs remained the same.

Figure 3.3. Risk management strategies and policies in Canada

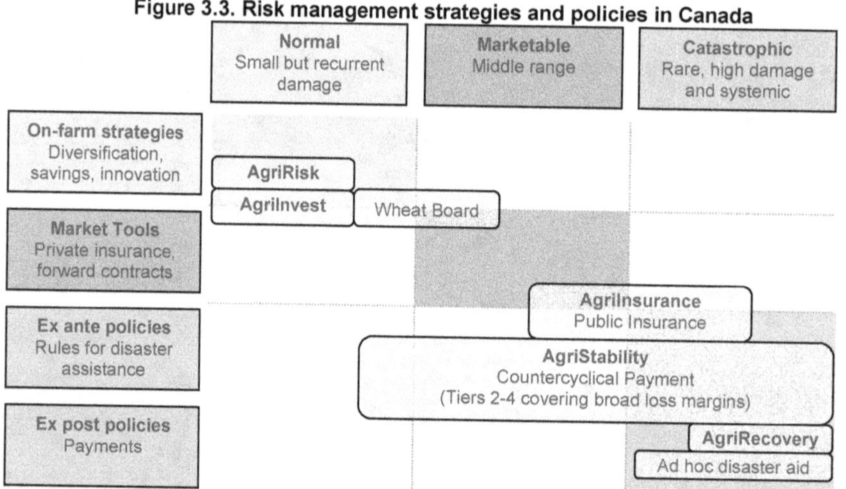

Source: Adapted from Antón, J., S. Kimura and R. Martini (2011), "Risk Management in Agriculture in Canada", *OECD Food, Agriculture and Fisheries Papers*, No. 40, OECD Publishing, http://dx.doi.org/10.1787/5kgj0d6189wg-en.

Additional risk management options are available at the Provincial and Territorial level. They complement existing Federal instruments. In Quebec, a collective-type Farm Income Stabilization Insurance (ASRA) protects producers against market and production cost fluctuations. Complementary to the AgriStability and AgriInvest programmes, ASRA pays compensation when the average selling price is lower than a stabilized income based on the production cost of specialized farm businesses. The Western Livestock Price Insurance Program (WLPIP website) protects livestock producers in British Columbia, Alberta, Saskatchewan and Manitoba against price fluctuations on cattle and hogs. Premiums are fully funded by producers. If the market price is lower than the insured price, a payment of the difference is made to producers. Hail insurance for Manitoba offers producers financial assistance for crop losses due to hail, accidental fire and, in some cases, frost (MASC website). Hail insurance is only available as complimentary insurance to AgriInsurance programme participants. Ontario's Risk Management Program (RMP website) helps producers manage risks in grains and oilseeds, cattle, hogs, sheep, veal and edible horticulture sectors. For grains and oilseeds, and livestock activities, payments are made when the commodity's average market price drops below the annual support level. For edible horticulture, government matching savings accounts help mitigate risk associated with farm business. Producers can enrol in RMP without participating in AgriStability.

Box 3.6. Crop risk management policy instruments in the US Farm Bill

The 2014 US Agricultural Act, also known as the Farm Bill, remains the cornerstone of US agricultural policy. The new Farm Bill introduces new policy instruments offering American producers options they can customise to manage their risk of shallow loss while also attempting to reduce agricultural support spending. Farmers' deep losses (below 75% of the benchmark indicator) are meant to be covered by a wide array of subsidised traditional crop insurance instruments, which are left largely unchanged from the previous Farm Bill. Through the Title I Commodity Programs, producers have a choice among an individual farm revenue programme the Agricultural Risk Coverage-Individual Coverage (ARC-IC), a county revenue programme the Agricultural Risk Coverage-County Level (ARC-CO) or a price-based programme the Price Loss Coverage (PLC). To facilitate farmers' decision-making, resources have been made available through USD 3 million awarded to land grant universities' developing web-based decision tools. At the time it was adopted, the US Congressional Budget Office (CBO) estimated that the Title I programmes would reduce public spending on commodity support by USD 14.3 billion and Title XI Crop Insurance costs by USD 5.7 billion over the 2014-23 period (CBO, 2014), but this remains to be confirmed. Based on the first year of payments, commodity programmes that were estimated to cost taxpayers USD 3.24 billion per year actually cost USD 5.02 billion (Smith, 2016 and CBO, 2016). Payments for 2015 crop production will be more than USD 7 billion. New forecasts with continued downward trending prices will trigger price support for commodities under Price Loss Coverage and may gradually lower benchmarks for support under Agricultural Risk Coverage (ARC-CO). With farm payments dependent largely on moving market prices, public budgets may need greater flexibility for annual variations on commodity payments although congressionally mandated automatic reductions through the Budget Control Act will already cut ARC and PLC payments by 6.8% for 2015.

The individual farm revenue programme, **Agricultural Risk Coverage (ARC-IC)** covers all commodities on the farm against shallow loss based on historical acres allocations and yields from 2008-12 data. The farm essentially establishes a benchmark for itself by which its future revenue will be measured against. Support occurs when the actual revenue for all the covered commodities on the farm is 86% to 76% of the benchmark revenue. Payments are capped in the event of steep losses. The ARC-IC cannot be combined with the **Supplemental Coverage Option (SCO)** crop insurance. Reporting requirements are heavy and payment calculation is complex. Regardless of commodity mix, less than 1% of farms have selected ARC-IC (FSA, 2016).

In the county revenue programme, **Agricultural Risk Coverage (ARC-CO)**, farms select revenue protection on a commodity-by-commodity basis. ARC-CO replaces the previous Farm Bill's state-based revenue programme, Average Crop Revenue Enhancement (ACRE). Commodity revenues are benchmarked against county revenues for each commodity, calculated using a moving 5-year Olympic average of county yields and national prices. Revenue payments are based on 85% of the covered commodity's base acres when county revenue is 86% to 76% below the benchmark county revenue, capped to be no more than 10% of the benchmarked revenue. High average county yields could eliminate payments and payments will likely vary among neighbouring counties. During the enrolment period, base reallocations for maize and soybeans increased the most by 12.8 million and 4.7 million acres and 90% of maize and soybean farms selected ARC-CO (FSA, 2016).

The price-based programme, **Price Loss Coverage (PLC)**, replaces the Countercyclical Payments programme, but with higher reference prices. PLC makes payments to producers (now at a rate of 85% of base acres) when market price for a commodity falls below the fixed reference price. PLC cannot be combined with ARC-CO for the selected commodity. Reference prices are fixed by legislation. For commodities covered under PLC, Supplemental Coverage Option is available to provide additional protection against yield loss. Over 90% of rice and peanut farms have selected PLC (FSA, 2016) as yield risk is less of concern with irrigation (Mercier, 2016).

Farmer choices between ARC-CO and PLC were based on farmer's expectation of price movement compared with programme yields. While choices for Title I commodity programmes are one time decisions for the life of Farm Bill, farmers can elect the supplemental crop insurance under Title XI on a yearly basis for commodities not covered by the ARC programme. Federal crop insurance programmes subsidise 65% of the premium paid by farmers for the individual private crop insurance policy they purchase. The **Supplemental Coverage Option (SCO)** provides expanded coverage against losses based on average county revenues. **The Stacked Income Protection Plan (STAX)** under Title XI covers upland cotton using the expected price for cotton rather than fixed reference prices as benchmark.

Overall, the combination of new commodity and crop insurance programmes of the 2014 Farm Bill with the renewed traditional yield and revenue insurance programmes from the previous Farm Bill has increased the focus of US farm support on payments to reduce revenue losses. This focus should lead to more stable farm incomes. Crop farmers can choose flexibly among different options to cover a wider range of losses but this greater flexibility might increase the complexity of the choice to be made. The crop reference prices set by the 2014 Farm Bill reflect high historical price levels in 2012-13 and create a higher safety net than in the past. Yet, the US farm safety net seems to provide better conditions to beginning farmers, and to the dairy and cotton sectors with customized support payments. Livestock producers are also not covered as extensively as crop farmers by the new Farm Bill.

3.2. Assessment of risk management in the CAP

Numerous factors influence risk management, their complexity is increased in the European Union as they involve multiple layers of governance and decision making. A holistic approach to risk management instruments extends beyond the traditional boundaries of agricultural policy, be it at national or European levels. Policy coherence is all the more decisive and before any new measures are set up under the CAP, it is important to avoid giving agricultural producers contradicting signals. Farming decisions should be market based and not prescribed by policies.

When policies set societal objectives and targets, producers should be offered the flexibility to decide the means to reach them. Efforts should be oriented to enable farmers' choices in developing their own production and risk management strategies. In this regard, policies have an important role to play in improving access to market information and to knowledge systems and facilitating compliance with regulatory frameworks.

From an EU agricultural policy making viewpoint, the inclusion of risk management tools in the RDPs anchors these measures in medium to long term planning and gives a positive signal to farmers in member states that choose to adopt such measures. Furthermore, the second pillar of the CAP offers more flexibility to adapt measures to local conditions. The impact of these measures can be increased if they are designed in conjunction with other measures that increase resilience, be it on farm such as the use of improved technology and inputs, drought resistant seeds and precision agriculture, and along the supply chain such as contracting and support for the constitution of farmer groups. The value of contracting, not only futures contracts, where available and suitable, but also production and marketing contracts, has been underlined. The latter are supported as part of the RDP priorities and their take-up has been encouraged. While the CAP has no authority for setting up an appropriate financial regulatory framework, it can target support to provide farmers with the necessary knowledge and advisory services to effectively use these financial instruments. Knowledge transmission and advisory services have been recognised to play a positive role in enabling farmers face risk.

The experience in Canada (Box 3.5) has shown that policies have been adapted through time to lessen the risk of crowding-out risk management systems. Federal and Provincial risk management schemes have been generally adapted to become complementary. The overlap between measures could be reduced by ensuring that each policy takes up a different level risk. However, the role of government remains prominent. In the United States, the Farm Bill 2014 offers multiple choices for similar levels of risk and overcrowding seems inevitable (Box 3.6). The system seems complex and budgetary needs are open ended.

The CAP risk management instruments do not operate in a vacuum and the low levels of member state take-up of the risk management measures, in terms of participation and budgets, can be interpreted in several ways. First, national preferences go to alternative uses of the CAP budgets instead of risk management measures. As explained earlier, a large share of public expenditure support is delivered through guaranteed payments and guarantees farmers a minimum income. This may lower the incentives to take up the specific risk management measures offered under the pillar 2 of the CAP. Second, alternative risk management instruments may be readily available and used domestically making CAP measures redundant (Box 3.1). In the case of the Netherlands and Spain, the juxtaposition of the two layers of national and European measures is illustrated in Figures 3.1 and 3.2 respectively. The Basic Payment Scheme offers a guaranteed income under all conditions. In addition to the BPS, the RDP of the Netherlands encompasses risk management instruments. In the case of Spain, both the risk management instruments and disaster prevention and restoration are included in regional RDP. Third, it could be that the institutional frameworks for private insurance and financial services that would offer the necessary services are not available. Addressing these shortfalls may require public regulatory intervention in member states and would fall beyond the boundaries of the CAP.

Effective risk management in EU agricultural policy requires an integrated approach that addresses all risk exposure and incentives, distinguishes between normal, marketable and catastrophic risk and articulates the respective roles of public authorities and economic actors, including them in the development of risk management strategies based on sound economic analysis of the three risk layers. Finally, while analysis has shown the importance of co-funding and co-responsibility of farmers in the sustainability of risk management systems, the incentives to take up such measures are low as long as farmers can assume that public assistance will be forthcoming in case of "exceptional circumstances". Defining "exceptional circumstances" and informing farmers of the conditions as well as of the modalities by which public assistance is delivered before risks materialise remains an important challenge for the design of effective risk management policies.

Notes

1.   Priority 3 is the overarching heading for Promoting food chain organisation, including processing and marketing of agricultural products, animal welfare and risk management in agriculture in the Regulation (EU) 1305/2013 on support for rural development (OJ, 2013a).

2.   Support to Knowledge transfer and information actions covers vocational training and skills acquisition as well as short term farm and forest management exchanges and visits.
Investments in physical assets covers: a) tangible and intangible investments which improve the overall performance and sustainability of the agricultural holding; b) concern the processing, marketing and development of agricultural products; c) concern infrastructure related to the development modernisation or adaptation of agriculture and forestry including access to farm and forest land, land consolidation etc.; or d) non-productive investments linked to the achievement of agri-environment-climate objectives.
Advisory services, farm management and farm relief services aim to: a) help farmers etc. benefit from advisory services for the improvement of the economic and environmental performance as well as the climate friendliness and resilience of their holding, enterprise etc.; b) promote the setting up of farm management, farm relief and farm advisory services etc.; and c) promote the training of advisors (OJ, 2013a).

3.   Disaster prevention and restoration is shorthand for Restoring agricultural production potential damaged by natural disaster and catastrophic events and introduction of appropriate prevention actions: it covers a) investments in preventive actions aimed at reducing the consequences of probable natural disasters, adverse climatic events and catastrophic events; and b) investments for the restoration of agricultural land and production potential (OJ, 2013a).

4.   The SAPS is applied in Cyprus*, Czech Republic, Estonia, Hungary, Latvia, Lithuania, Poland, Slovakia, Bulgaria, Romania. The BPS is applied in Slovenia, Malta, Croatia in addition to the EU15. A regional BPS is applied by Greece, Spain, Finland, Germany, France, in the United Kingdom (England) and in the United Kingdom (Scotland).

*Note by Turkey: The information in this document with reference to "Cyprus" relates to the southern part of the Island. There is no single authority representing both Turkish and Greek Cypriot people on the Island. Turkey recognises the Turkish Republic of Northern Cyprus (TRNC). Until a lasting and equitable solution is found within the context of the United Nations, Turkey shall preserve its position concerning the "Cyprus issue".

*Note by all the European Union Member States of the OECD and the European Union: The Republic of Cyprus is recognised by all members of the United Nations with the exception of Turkey. The information in this document relates to the area under the effective control of the Government of the Republic of Cyprus.

5.   http://ec.europa.eu/growth/sectors/food/competitiveness/supply-chain-forum_en.

6.   http://www.supplychaininitiative.eu/.

References

Antón, J. and S. Kimura (2011), "Risk Management in Agriculture in Spain", *OECD Food, Agriculture and Fisheries Papers*, No. 43, OECD Publishing, Paris, http://dx.doi.org/10.1787/5kgj0d57w0wd-en.

CBO (2016), "CBO's March 2016 Baseline for Farm Programs", US Congressional Business Office, www.cbo.gov/sites/default/files/recurringdata/51317-2016-03-usda.pdf.

CBO (2014), Estimated Budgetary Effects HR 2642 Agricultural Act of 2014.

Cordier (2014), Comparative analysis of risk management tools supported by the 2014 Farm Bill and the CAP 2014-2020, European Parliament, Brussels.

EC (2016) Press release http://europa.eu/rapid/press-release_IP-16-2563_en.htm.

FSA (2016), "ARC/PLC Election Data", USDA Farm Service Agency, https://www.fsa.usda.gov/Assets/USDA-FSA-Public/usdafiles/arc-plc/excel/arc_plc_election_data.xlsx.

Government of Ireland, Department of Finance (2016), Budget 2017, http://www.budget.gov.ie/Budgets/2017/Documents/Getting%20Ireland%20Brexit%20Ready_final.pdf

Keogh, M., R. Granger and S. Middleton (2011), *Drought Pilot Review Panel: a review of the pilot of drought reform measures in Western Australia,* Canberra, A.C.T., www.agriculture.gov.au/SiteCollectionDocuments/ag-food/drought/wa-droughtpilot-review.pdf.

Melyukhina, O. (2011), "Risk Management in Agriculture in the Netherlands", *OECD Food, Agriculture and Fisheries Papers*, No. 41, OECD Publishing, Paris, http://dx.doi.org/10.1787/5kgj0d5lqn48-en.

Mercier, S. (2016) "A new paradigm for US farm programs", *Farm Journal Foundation,* www.agchallenge2050.org/farm-and-food-policy/2014/11/a-new-paradigm-for-us-farm-programs/.

OECD (2016a), *Agricultural Policy Monitoring and Evaluation 2016*, OECD Publishing, Paris, http://dx.doi.org/10.1787/agr_pol-2016-en.

OECD (2016b), "Producer and Consumer Support Estimates", OECD Agriculture Statistics (database), http://dx.doi.org/10.1787/agr-pcse-data-en.

OECD (2011), *Managing risk in Agriculture – Policy assessment and design,* OECD Publishing, Paris, http://dx.doi.org/10.1787/9789264116146-en.

OECD (2009), *Managing Risk in Agriculture: A Holistic Approach*, OECD Publishing, Paris, http://dx.doi.org/10.1787/9789264075313-en.

Official Journal of the European Union (OJ) (2016a), Delegated Regulation (EU) 2016/1614 laying down temporary exceptional measures for the milk and milk products sector in the form of extending the public intervention period for skimmed milk powder in 2016 and advancing the public intervention period for skimmed milk powder in 2017, Brussels.

OJ (2016b) Commission Delegated Regulation (EU) 2016/558 authorising agreements and decisions of cooperatives and other forms of producer organisations in the milk and milk products sector on the planning of production, Brussels.

OJ (2015a), Commission Regulation (EU) 2015/1549 laying down temporary exceptional measures for the milk and milk product sector in the form of extending the public intervention period for butter and skimmed milk powder in 2015 and advancing the public intervention period for butter and skimmed milk powder in 2016, Brussels.

OJ (2015b) Commission Delegated Regulation (EU) 2015/1853 providing for temporary exceptional aid to farmers in the livestock sectors, Brussels.

OJ (2014) Commission Delegated Regulation (EU) No 1336/2014 laying down temporary exceptional measures for the milk and milk product sector in the form of advancing the public intervention period for butter and skimmed milk powder in 2015, Brussels.

OJ (2013a), Regulation (EU) No 1305/2013 of the European Parliament and of the Council on support for rural development by the European Agricultural Fund for Rural Development (EAFRD), Brussels.

OJ (2013b) Regulation (EU) No 1308/2013 of the European Parliament and of the Council establishing a common organisation of the markets in agricultural products), Brussels.

Smith, VH (2016), "A Midterm Review of the 2014 Farm Bill", American Enterprise Institute, www.aei.org/wp-content/uploads/2016/02/Midterm-Review.format.pdf.

Websites

AAFC (2016), Report on plans and priorities, www.agr.gc.ca/eng/about-us/planning-and-reporting/reports-on-plans-and-priorities/2016-17-report-on-plans-and-priorities/?id=1455737253940.

ASRA – Quebec, www.fadq.qc.ca/en/stabilization-insurance/description/.

GF2, Growing forward 2: A Federal - Provincial - Territorial framework agreement on Agriculture, Agri-food and Agri-based products policy, www.agr.gc.ca/eng/about-us/key-departmental-initiatives/growing-forward-2/?id=1294780620963.

MASC, Hail insurance – Manitoba, www.masc.mb.ca/masc.nsf/program_hail.html.

RMP - Ontario, www.agricorp.com/en-ca/Programs/RMP/Cattle/Pages/Overview.aspx.

WLPIP, www.wlpip.ca/about.

Chapter 4

Environmental components

Through time, the CAP has developed a range of policy measures that address environmental issues in agriculture. EU farmers are required to adopt certain practices deemed to deliver particular environmental outcomes. A number of voluntary schemes are also available for take up by EU farmers. The CAP 2014-20 introduced a new greening payment with more stringent requirements. This chapter describes the environmental components of the CAP 2014-20 and discusses whether they are innovative or rather represent a continuation of previous policies. The chapter offers an ex ante assessment of the potential impacts of these measures that is based on a review of the literature, on the results of the CAPRI model of European agriculture and on the analysis of farm support using the PSE framework.

4.1. Background

Agriculture is a major user of natural resources such as land and water; it influences eco-systems and biodiversity and shapes rural landscapes. It has a complex relationship with the environment: it creates greenhouse gas emissions but also acts as carbon sink, it has a potential to foster or harm ecosystems (biodiversity); can be considered as a provider of cultural landscapes but also as a polluter of natural resources (land, water). In 2014, agriculture used roughly 44% of its land area and accounted for 26% of total water abstractions in the European Union (OECD, 2016).

The EU Common Agricultural Policy (CAP), combined with environmental regulations,[1] require farmers – either at their own costs or with public support – to adopt certain practices deemed to deliver particular environmental outcomes.

Through time, the CAP has developed a range of policy measures that address environmental issues in agriculture. This chapter focuses on such measures in the CAP 2014-20 and assesses whether they are innovative or rather represent a continuation of previous policies. The following measures are covered: Greening; Agri-environment and climate measures; organic farming; Natura 2000 and Water Framework Directive payments.

4.2. Description of environmental components of the CAP

The general framework of the greening payment

Greening is a new measure introduced in the budgetary package for 2014-20. In 2016, it took up 31% of the direct payments budget, or 36% of the decoupled direct payments' budget. By way of comparison, the Basic Payment Scheme took up 40% of the direct payments' budget (Table 4.1). Greening requires farmers to implement specific farming practices. These come in addition to existing compulsory environmental cross-compliance and its standards for good agricultural and environmental conditions (GAEC) that are attached to most payments (cross-compliance is described in Box 4.2). More stringent requirements are attached to the greening payment, while flexibility exists to adapt or waive those additional requirements.

Table 4.1. Direct payments budget

	2016 appropriations (EUR million)	Share in direct payments	Share in decoupled direct payments
Direct payments; of which:	39 446		
Decoupled direct payments; of which:	34 269	87%	
BPS	15 927	40%	46%
SAPS	4 237	11%	12%
Greening	12 239	31%	36%

Source: Budget data are sourced in EUR-Lex budget 2017, http://eur-lex.europa.eu/budget/data/DB/2017/en/SEC03.pdf (accessed on 28 February 2017).

More specifically, in order to receive the *greening* payment farmers have to comply with the following requirements (EC regulation 1307/2013):

Ecological Focus Area: Holdings with more than 15 hectares of arable land must manage at least 5% of their arable land as Ecological Focus Area (EFA). Subject to approval by co-legislators, the ratio is to increase to 7% by 2017. Holdings with specific farming practices, notably grassland, are exempt. The following elements qualify as EFA: land lying fallow; terraces, nine different types of landscape features, buffer strips, areas of agro-forestry, strips of eligible land along forest edges (with or without production), areas with short rotation coppice (18 species), afforested areas, areas with catch crops or green cover and areas with nitrogen fixing crops (24 crops).

Permanent Grassland: Member states must maintain the ratio of permanent grassland to total agricultural area, defined at national or regional level, at not less than 95% of their reference level combining permanent pastures declared in 2012 and additional permanent grassland declared in 2015. If the ratio falls below this threshold, permanent grassland converted to other uses must be reconverted to grassland.

Crop diversification: Holdings with more than 10 hectares of arable land must grow at least two crops, where the main crop cannot cover more than 75% of the arable land. For holdings larger than 30 hectares, that is for 62% of EU arable land, a third crop must be cultivated at least and the two main crops cannot cover more than 95% of the land. Exemptions apply, for example for holdings where the arable land is entirely cultivated with crops under water for a significant part of the year and for holdings with more than 75% of their land under grass, forage or fallow. Rotation may be implemented instead of diversification under certain conditions.

No conditions are attached to greening payments for participants in the small farmers scheme (5% of EU agricultural area), for farms with less than 10 hectares of land, for organic farms and for areas under permanent crops (6% of the total EU agricultural area) (OJ, 2016).

Implementation of greening by member states

Member states and, to a lesser degree, farmers are given some flexibility in deciding the menu of instruments used to meet the three requirements. Equivalent practices are allowed that can replace the three initial conditions. Annex 4.A2 gives a detailed list of member states' implementation choices of greening requirements. A recent study of the implementation of greening in Sweden has evaluated the environmental benefits induced by changes in farming practices at EUR 1.5 per hectare, while the expected transaction costs have also been estimated at EUR 1.5 per hectare, resulting in a null net effect (Söderberg, 2016).

The Ecological Focus Area (EFA) condition offers member states flexibility to choose from a menu of features established at the European Union level. In turn, farmers may select from their member state menu the features they implement.

The Ecological Focus Area (EFA) currently concerns 3.7 million hectares of arable area, which represents 4.5% of total EU arable area.[2] The most popular EFA features include areas with nitrogen-fixing crops, fallow land, landscape features and areas with short rotation coppice and catch crops or green cover. The positive impacts of some features on the environment are greater and their adoption is deemed to deliver the greatest positive impact of greening (Söderberg, 2016). However, a recent study estimates that "only 26.9% of the physical area of EFA was devoted to the most beneficial elements for the environment" (EC, 2016). In addition, some of these elements are already part of the cross-compliance GAEC standards and would not require changing farming practices.

The condition related to the maintenance of Permanent Grasslands allows member states to choose whether to apply this requirement at national or regional level. Member states may designate a number of Environmentally Sensitive Permanent Grassland areas, both in areas covered by the EU birds and habitats Directives (Natura 2000 network) and outside such areas. Not all permanent grassland within a Natura 2000 site must be designated as Environmentally Sensitive Permanent Grassland.

Most member states, except four (Belgium, France, Germany and the United Kingdom), have chosen to apply the permanent grassland condition at the national level. Member states' choices as to the designation of Environmentally Sensitive Permanent Grassland in Natura 2000 areas are quite diverse, while ten member states[3] have designated all grassland within the Natura 2000 network as Environmentally Sensitive Permanent Grassland, the ratio is below 50% for 11 other members (Annex 4.A2 for more details).

As a result of the EU farm structure, crop diversification applies to 75% of total EU arable land and crop diversification is a customary practice on most farms (EC, 2016). In relative terms, farms specialised in field crops are most affected by the measure and need to adapt their agricultural practices to comply with the crop diversification requirement. In absolute terms, 67% of the farms that need to apply diversification are farms specialised in field crops, representing 68% of the land area subject to diversification. Moreover, areas that have to be diversified in order to comply with the requirement are mainly cropped with wheat, maize and barley, followed by oats, sunflower, rye and potatoes. In practice, the cultivated crop was changed on 1% of total EU arable land as a result of crop diversification requirements (EC, 2016).

Equivalent practices for crop diversification include: (i) more demanding crop diversification: at least four crops, lower ceilings, a more appropriate selection of crops; (ii) crop rotation: a more environmentally beneficial multiannual sequence of crops or fallow; (iii) sowing a winter soil cover; and (iv) sowing catch crops.

Four member states, Austria, France, Ireland and Poland have implemented an equivalent practice. Arable land subject to crop diversification that is under an equivalent practice amounts to 0.2% in Ireland, 1.6% in Poland and 62% in Austria. In Austria, about 48% of farmers subject to the requirement apply an equivalent practice, while the ratio falls to 1% in Poland and to 0.3% in Ireland (Annex 4.A2).

The general framework of environmental measures in the Rural Development Programmes

In addition to greening, policy measures addressing environmental issues in agriculture are developed within member states' Rural Development Programmes (RDP) financed from pillar 2 and co-financed by member states (Chapter 2, Box 2.2). Several member states (Belgium, Finland, France, Germany, Italy, Portugal, and Spain) developed RDPs at regional levels (Annex 4.A2). In most countries, the regional approach follows the administrative organisation of the national territory and regions are not defined according to their specific environmental characteristics.

In the CAP 2014-20 at least 30% of RDP expenditure should go to environment and climate related measures, from a list of measures related to agriculture and forestry. The measures include investment in the environment and climate, the development of woodland and improving the viability of forests, "agri-environment-climate" measures, organic farming and payments under Natura 2000. In the CAP 2007-13 the minimum expenditure on measures deemed to improve the environment and the countryside was fixed at 25%.

Agri-environment and climate measures

Agri-environment and climate (AEC) measures are available throughout the territories of member states and aim to preserve and promote the necessary changes to agricultural practices that make a positive contribution to the environment and climate. AEC payments are granted to farmers who undertake, on a voluntary basis, operations consisting of one or more agri-environment-climate commitments on agricultural land. An AEC payment covers only those commitments going beyond the relevant mandatory standards (environmental regulation, environmental cross-compliance, greening requirements). The participation in the programme is set for five to seven years and the payments are made on an annual basis.

The characteristics of AEC measures are similar to those of Agri-environmental payments provided to farmers within the previous policy set applied for 2007-13 and also in the preceding period. There are no fundamental changes in the implementation of these payments. In terms of the PSE classification M10 AEC payments are mostly classified in category C – payments based on area/animal numbers. Some M04 payments for investments in physical assets are related to landscape development and fall under agri-environment and climate measures; these payments are categorised as F – payments based on non-commodity criteria (Chapter 2, Box 2.3). All those payments (across all categories) are bearing the label "voluntary constraints – environment".

Organic farming

This measure provides support in the form of payments per hectare of agricultural area to farmers who convert to, or maintain, on a voluntary basis, organic farming practices and methods defined in Council Regulation EC No 834/2007. As is the case for the Agri-environment-climate payments, support is only granted for commitments going beyond the relevant mandatory standards. There is virtually no change concerning the regulations set for organic farming compared with 2007-13, although the CAP 2014-20 identifies support to organic farming as a distinct measure. In the PSE classification M11 payments for organic farming are in category C – payments based on area, with a label "voluntary constraints – environment".

Natura 2000 and Water Framework Directive payments

Support is granted annually per hectare of agricultural area or per hectare of forest in order to compensate beneficiaries for additional cost and income foregone resulting from additional constraints applied in the areas concerned (Natura 2000 areas and areas defined within the Water Framework Directive). There is virtually no change concerning the regulations set for those payments compared with 2007-13. Within the PSE classification, payments to the forestry sector are excluded and only payments per hectare of agricultural land are included in the measurement of agriculture support and are classified as payment per area (category C) with a label "compulsory input constraints".

Other RDP payments not directly related to environmental issues in agriculture

Other important payments are granted to farmers within the national or regional RDPs. More specifically these are *Payments to areas facing natural or other specific constraints* and payments for *Animal welfare*. In many national programmes the payments to areas facing natural or other constraints are one of the most important in terms of budgetary expenditures, while payments for animal welfare are relatively modest compared with the AEC payments.

Implementation of Rural Development programmes by member states

Agri-environment and climate measures

On average the main spendings in the approved RDPs support investments in agriculture (23% of total RDPs spending) followed by agri-environment and climate measures (AECM) and Areas with Natural Constraints expenditures with respectively 19% and 16% of total spending (Chapter 2). As the priorities differ across member states, the share of expenditure related to the AECM in total RDP varies (Table 4.2). This share ranges from 5% in Croatia and Malta to 49% in the United Kingdom. In addition to the United Kingdom, there are five other member states where the share is close to or above 30% (Ireland, the Netherlands, Austria, the Czech Republic and Luxembourg). The share is below 10% in eight member states.

Box 4.1. Agri-environment and climate measures: decentralised implementation in France

EU member states have the possibility to decentralise the implementation of Agri-environment and climate measures (AECM) of the new CAP's Rural Development Programme (RDP). France has chosen to delegate AECM priority setting, programming, implementing of funding commitments, and monitoring and evaluation to local government at regional level, the *Conseil régional,* in the 18 administrative regions in France.

While the entire AECM is decentralised, the regional strategy must be consistent with the national RDP framework, which was also approved by the European Commission. The national framework contains the exhaustive list of measures that can be used in regional RDPs and defines the modalities of their implementation. At the national level, France has defined three objectives for its RDP framework, under which, regions can select policy instruments to fulfil AECM requirements: diversifying farming system combinations, addressing local issues and improving genetic biodiversity. The measures addressing the first two objectives are so-called "zoned operations" because they are linked to a specific territory where the issue is relevant. Measures to improve genetic biodiversity are not geographically restricted.

As part of the decentralised RDP management set out by France, authority for the RDP lies with the *Conseil régional,* hereafter *Région*. The *Région* selects its RDP priorities in line with the national RDP framework. Before implementing any AECM project, a regional AECM commission of local and national rural development experts is set up. It is co-presided by the *Région* and a representative of the national government. It serves as an advisory board that helps select AECM contracts. This regional AECM commission is consulted every year to give its expert opinion on the monitoring of on-going projects.

The AECM "zoned operations" related to diversifying farming system combinations and addressing local issues can only be implemented through an agri-environment-climate project (AECP). Each AECP lasts in general two to three years. Once a farmer has engaged in an AECM, the commitments are undertaken for a period of five years. In all cases, an AECP must be submitted and implemented, on a voluntary basis, by a project holder: a structure federating stakeholders within the territory and embodying a collective territorial dynamic. Project holders can be farmers, farmers' groups or other land managers, and they must be qualified in agronomy, environment, economics and project management.

AECM payments are only granted to farmers for their committed hectares. Therefore if the project holder is an institution, it is only implementing the project while participating farmers receive the AECM payments. These annual payments compensate farmers for all or part of the additional costs and income foregone resulting from the commitments made. When necessary, payments may also cover transaction costs for up to 20% of the payments. Where commitments are undertaken by groups of farmers or groups of farmers and other land managers, additional payments valued at up to 30% of the payments made to farmers can be provided to cover transaction costs.

Annex 4.A1 provides a more detailed description of the decentralised implementation of AECMs in the Centre-Val de Loire region of France.

Organic farming

This support is provided in all member states except the Netherlands and the share of payments to organic farming in total RDP spending varies from 1% to 11% (Table 4.2). All member states have developed the rules for the marketing of organic products including the certification and labels informing consumers (Rousset et al., 2015). There is a functioning market for these products. Current support covers both transitional aid to those producers who switch from conventional production to organic but also to maintain organic farming production.

Table 4.2. Agri-environment-climate measures and organic farming expenditure by member state

Public expenditure, including co-financing (EUR million)	AEC	Organic farming	Total public expenditure for rural development (sum of EU and national funding)	Share of AEC in total RD expenditure (%)	Share of OF in total RD expenditure (%)
Austria	2 239	785	7 812	29	10
Belgium	347	110	1 579	22	7
Bulgaria	223	152	2 918	8	5
Croatia	139	128	2 383	6	5
Cyprus	60	14	243	25	6
Czech Republic	905	331	3 074	29	11
Denmark	189	111	907	21	12
Estonia	245	78	993	25	8
Finland	1 601	331	8 325	19	4
France	1 820	793	16 985	11	5
Germany	3 279	1 617	16 886	19	10
Greece	472	801	5 880	8	14
Hungary	638	208	4 174	15	5
Ireland	1 588	56	3 916	41	1
Italy	2 518	1 689	20 925	12	8
Latvia	112	152	1 532	7	10
Lithuania	142	151	1 978	7	8
Luxembourg	110	7	368	30	2
Malta	7	0	130	5	0
Netherlands	496	No expenditure	1 645	30	/
Poland	1 184	700	13 513	9	5
Portugal	562	99	4 721	12	2
Roumania	1 071	236	9 473	11	2
Slovakia	144	90	2 080	7	4
Slovenia	204	60	1 107	18	5
Spain	1 383	673	13 155	11	5
Sweden	963	491	4 300	22	11
United Kingdom	3 718	85	7 626	49	1
Average across EU28				17	6

Notes: AECM: Agri-environment-climate measures, OF: organic farming, RD: Rural development.

Note by Turkey: The information in this document with reference to "Cyprus" relates to the southern part of the Island. There is no single authority representing both Turkish and Greek Cypriot people on the Island. Turkey recognises the Turkish Republic of Northern Cyprus (TRNC). Until a lasting and equitable solution is found within the context of the United Nations, Turkey shall preserve its position concerning the "Cyprus issue".

Note by all the European Union Member States of the OECD and the European Union: The Republic of Cyprus is recognised by all members of the United Nations with the exception of Turkey. The information in this document relates to the area under the effective control of the Government of the Republic of Cyprus.

Source: OECD calculations based on national 2014-20 RDP budget as published in: http://ec.europa.eu/agriculture/rural-development-2014-2020/country-files/index_en.htm, 2016.

Trends and share of environmental payments in agricultural support

Both Agri-environment-climate payments (previously agri-environmental payments) and payments for organic farming are granted to farmers within programmes adopted by farmers on a voluntary basis (in contrast to compulsory environmental cross-compliance, compulsory greening and payments for agricultural land in Natura 2000 areas). Hence, these payments can be identified and aggregated in the PSE database using the label *voluntary constraints – environment*. Apart from the EU, Switzerland and the United States also use such payments on a large scale and since a relatively long period of time (Box 4.2). Figure 4.1 shows the trend of these payments within the last ten years. While the level of these payments in the EU28 and the United States is rather flat, the latest reform in Switzerland has increased the level of such payments within an overall stable budget, thus leading to some changes in the composition of support (OECD, 2015).

Box 4.2. Mandatory minimum environmental requirements and voluntary adoption of more stringent constraints: Examples from the European Union, Switzerland and the United States

It is important to note that while payments may be conditional to mandatory minimum environmental requirements or to voluntary and more stringent constraints, support delivered through market protection has no such conditions attached.

Mandatory and voluntary environmental requirements attached to agricultural support in the European Union

Mandatory environmental requirements

The European Union's direct payments under the CAP are typically conditional on mandatory cross-compliance. In this context, cross-compliance refers to environment, climate change and good agricultural condition of land as well as public, animal and plant health, and animal welfare. It applies to direct payments and environmental RDP payments. Cross-compliance applies to all agricultural land including land which is left fallow and no longer used for production purposes. Cross-compliance obligations are waived for small farms and national programmes that are not CAP related.

Cross-compliance combines so-called Statutory Management Requirements (SMR) that relate to the implementation of legislative standards in the field of the environment, food safety, animal and plant health and animal welfare (18 EU Directives and Regulations) and the standards for Good Agricultural and Environmental Condition of land (GAEC). Adjustments were made in the CAP 2014-20 to the conditions of cross-compliance.

GAEC standards define minimum agricultural management practices addressing water quality, soil cover and erosion, biodiversity, conservation of habitats, flora and fauna and landscape features. GAEC standards establish buffer strips along water courses, minimum soil cover and land management to limit erosion, maintenance of soil organic matter level, retention of landscape features.

As described in detail in section 4.3, the greening payment conditions are compulsory and more stringent than cross-compliance. The regulation foresees that if the conditions are not fulfilled the payment is disrupted and penalties may apply. Payments under the Natura 2000 and Water framework directive are also associated with compulsory environmental requirements that are imposed on farmers and land owners under these areas.

Voluntary environmental conditions

Some RDP programmes provide payments compensating the application of more stringent conditions attached that go beyond mandatory standards and requirements. Farmers who apply for the programme adhere to these conditions on a voluntary basis. These include the agri-environment and climate payments, the organic farming and animal welfare payments.

Source: EU Regulation 1306/2013, Chapter I of Title VI; and EU Regulation 1305/2013 Title III, articles 28, 29 and 30.

Mandatory minimum environmental requirements and voluntary adoption of more stringent constraints: Switzerland

Since 1999, Swiss farms need to fulfil the criteria of the Proof of Ecological Performance (PEP) in order to be eligible for direct payments. PEP rules are defined in Article 70 of the Federal Law on Agriculture.

The main PEP criteria are:

Balanced nutrient use: maximum 10% surplus of nitrogen and phosphorus as shown by a farm's nutrient balance (based on crop requirements).

Minimum share of ecological compensation areas (ECA): at least 7% of a farm's utilised agricultural area has to be allocated as ecological compensation area (e.g. extensive meadows, low intensity pastures, traditional orchards, hedgerows, wild flower strips, and low intensity cropping strips).

Establish buffer strips along water courses and forests *Crop rotation*: at least four different crops have to be cultivated per year on those farms where arable land area exceeds 3 ha and maximum shares of individual crops must be respected.

Soil protection: field parcels that are harvested before 31 August must be sown with main or cover crops subsequently so that periodical soil erosion is minimized.

Targeted application of pesticides: restrictions on the use and timing of various herbicides and insecticides, consideration of early warning systems and pest forecasts, frequent tests of sprayers.

Animal welfare: farm animals have to be kept according to legal requirements (compliance with the animal protection ordinance).

Ecological direct payments are another category of newly introduced direct payments during the 1990s reforms (together with the general direct payments). These payments are provided to farmers who volunteer within programmes with more stringent constraints to farm activities. These payments are designed to provide additional remuneration to farmers for activities supporting biodiversity; improving landscape, animal welfare; some of the programmes provide incentives for more sustainable use of resources and to reduce pollution. Overall, the sum of the ecological direct payments is much lower, compared to the general direct payments, but these payments recorded a continuous upward trend in the period 1993-2013, which reflects increasing participation of farmers in those programmes and a larger choice of programmes becoming available. The role of the ecological direct payments increased further in the agricultural policy programmes applied in 2014-27.

More details on Swiss agricultural policies can be found in OECD (2015).

Environmental cross-compliance of agricultural subsidies in the United States

At the federal level, the United States operates two types of agri-environmental programmes – mandatory conservation compliance for participants in most farm programmes, and voluntary conservation programmes that may involve land rental, cost-share for implementation of conservation practices, and incentive payments.

Most farm programmes, including commodity programmes (income support), crop insurance premium subsidies, and conservation payments are conditional on mandatory cross-compliance requirements since 1985. As a result, nearly all US farm support is tied to some environmental cross-compliance. Environmental cross-compliance in the US consists of targeted environmental stewardship tools tailored to highly erodible cropland and wetlands, which differs from the European Union and Swiss models. Requirements were suspended in 1996 and reinstated by the 2014 Farm Bill. Farmers must apply soil conservation systems (one or more practices designed to reduce soil erosion) on highly erodible cropland in order to receive support. Wetlands drainage is not allowed on farms located in designated wetland areas.

Voluntary conservation programmes promote: 1) farmland retirement; 2) environmentally sound production practices on working farmland; and 3) agricultural land preservation against residential or commercial development. The 2014 Farm Bill consolidated the number of voluntary programmes while keeping most previous conservation options and incorporating elements of all three types of programmes. The Conservation Reserve Program (CRP), for example, offers 10-15 year contracts to remove environmentally sensitive land, including wetlands, from agricultural production and maintain it with conservation practices, such as grass or tree cover, as well as providing riparian easements and support for other long-term partial field retirements.

The Agricultural Conservation Easement Program (ACEP) offers land preservation options including long term or permanent easements for the preservation of grasslands and the protection of agricultural land from commercial or residential development, as well as support for land retirement to restore wetlands on working land. The Environmental Quality Incentives Program (EQIP) provides financial assistance to farmers who adopt or install conservation practices on land in agricultural production, including livestock production. The Conservation Stewardship Program (CSP) supports ongoing and new conservation efforts for producers who meet stewardship requirements on working agricultural and forest lands. The Regional Conservation Partnership Program (RCPP) essentially promotes new institutional mechanisms designed to coordinate conservation programme assistance with public and private partners to solve environmental problems involving the agricultural sector on a regional or watershed scale.

Figure 4.1. Total Agri-environmental payments[a] in selected OECD countries

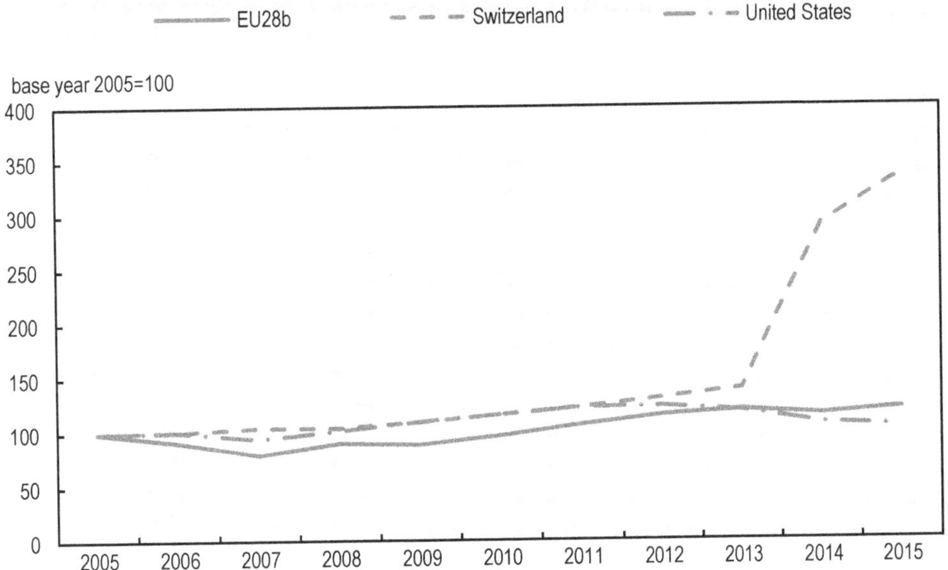

Notes: a) Agri-environmental payments used in this figure provide support to farmers for undertaking on a voluntary basis farming practices designed to achieve specific environmental objectives that go beyond environmental regulation (including cross-compliance) requirements. Farm support related to environmental cross-compliance and payments to disadvantaged areas are not included.
b) Payments for EU28 in 2015 were estimated using budget information on pillar 2 Rural Development Programmes.

Source: OECD (2016a), Producer and Consumer Support Estimates and OECD calculations based on national 2014-20 RDP budget as published in: http://ec.europa.eu/agriculture/rural-development-2014-2020/country-files/index_en.htm, 2016.

When tracking the shares of EU28 producer support estimate with input constraints (both compulsory and voluntary) along the different CAP reform cycles (Figure 4.2.a), two main conclusions can be drawn. Over the long-term, the share of producer support tied to environmental constraints, mandatory and voluntary, has grown to reach an average 60% of the total EU PSE in 2014-15. This indicates the growing importance of environmental payments within the European Union's agricultural support. The PSE since the 2013 reform saw a slight increase in the share of producer support with no constraint and a concurrent decrease in the share of producer support with mandatory constraints. This shift was due to a higher 2015 market price support estimate resulting from an increase of EU-level average domestic prices in a context of lower world prices. When including delayed RDP payments (pillar 2), the share of payments to farmers associated with voluntary environmental constraints (AEC payments, payments to organic farming) has increased by 1 percentage point, from 9% to 10%.

As illustrated in Figure 4.2.b, although the share of support delivered with no constraints has decreased through time, such support makes up more than 60% of national expenditure in EU member states that are accounted for in the PSE calculations for the European Union.

From a farm support point of view, the size of greening payments is proportionate to the size of the land holding. It relates neither to the expected environmental benefits, nor to the additional compliance costs borne by farmers, nor to the compensation of income foregone.

As such, greening payments are classified in the PSE in the same way as the basic payment scheme and the single area payment scheme; they are labelled as payments with compulsory input constraints. The qualitative change is in the level of compulsory requirements for the greening payments.

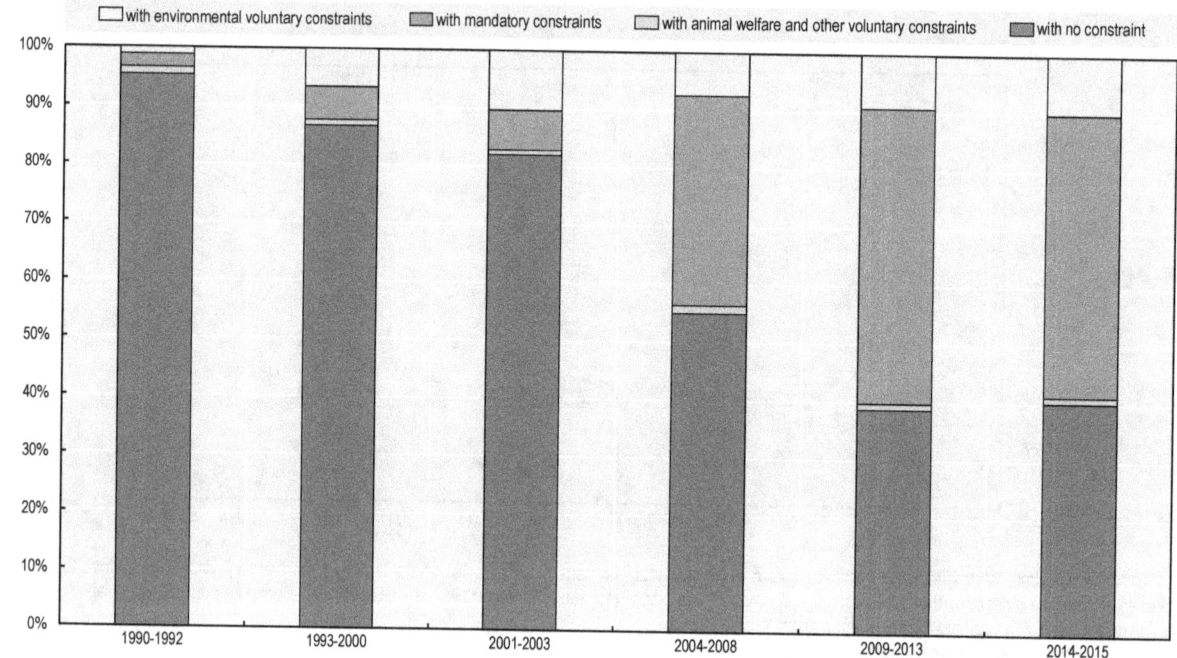

Figure 4.2.a. EU producer support details of input constraints conditions

Note: Data for 2014-15 has been adjusted to take into account budget information on pillar 2 Rural Development Programmes.

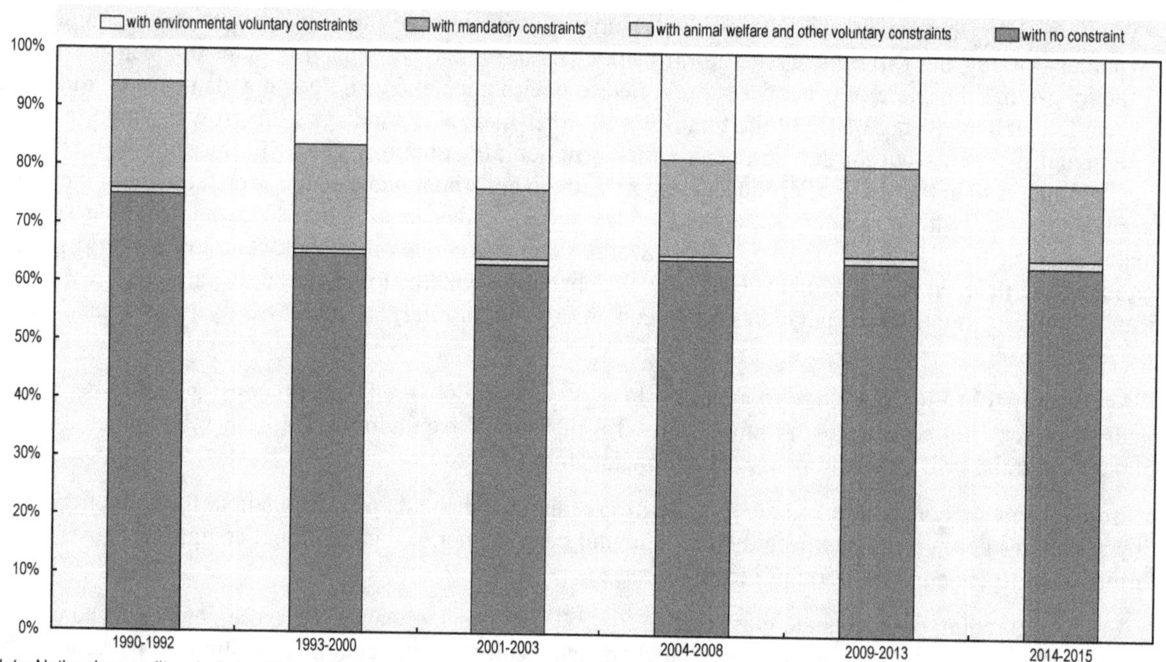

Figure 4.2.b. National expenditure in the EU producer support details of input constraints conditions

Note: National expenditure includes CAP co-funding of pillar 2 measures and national top-ups as well as national budget expenditure on agriculture as defined in the PSE framework.

Source: OECD (2016a) "Characteristics of Policy Support", OECD Agriculture Statistics (database) http://stats.oecd.org/viewhtml.aspx?QueryId=70972&vh=0000&vf=0&l&il=&lang=en and OECD calculations based on national 2014-20 RDP budget as published in: http://ec.europa.eu/agriculture/rural-development-2014-2020/country-files/index_en.htm, 2016.

4.3.   Assessment of the environmental components of the CAP

As described above the greening payment introduces new features in the CAP, while other measures represent a continuation of existing measures under previous CAP. This section endeavours to give a detailed assessment of the greening payment and concludes with a general assessment of the environmental dimension of the CAP.

The greening payment

As it is too early for an *ex post* evaluation of the greening measures, Box 4.3 summarises the results of a review of studies that assess initial observations and foresee the potential impacts of the greening measures. In addition the CAPRI model was used to simulate the impact of the CAP 2014-20 on land allocation (animal herd size), production, producer prices and trade. It estimates the changes in these components induced by the CAP 2014-20 against a reference scenario where measures of the CAP 2007-13 would have been continued until 2020 (Box 2.4. and Annex 2.A1).

Using CAPRI the comparison of changes from the reference scenario with the scenario of the full CAP 2014-20 implementation and the scenario without the greening payment suggests that, generally, the effects of greening are aligned with those of the CAP 2014-20 and most estimated changes are less than 1% when aggregated to the EU28 level.

Box 4.3. Literature on the potential effects of the greening payment on the environment

Through the greening payment additional environmental conditions have been imposed on payments that would have otherwise been only conditional on, perceived, less stringent cross-compliance.

Actual effects of the greening payment will depend largely on the specific implementation in each member states. The nature of the impacts depends on the type, location and management at farm level. For example, while nitrogen-fixing crops have been chosen by most European Union member states as part of the Ecological Focus Area (EFA), the management of crops may lead to different results and effects can be either positive or negative (Hart and Radley, 2016).

Regarding farm practices, the EFA obligation to idle some additional land would lead to more land area not being ploughed, but might increase intensive practices on land remaining under production (Pelikan et al., 2015). A case study on the use and intensity of fertilizer on Utilised Agricultural Area (UAA) in Austria before and after the reform concludes to diverging impact of the reform depending on local conditions (Kirchner et al., 2015).

The impacts of crop diversification on biodiversity are likely to be very limited, because most European farmers already grow two to three different crops and thus have already met this requirement. The effects of this measure will only impact specialised agricultural areas, covered by large-scale monocultures, and limit the likely impact to only 2% of EU arable area (Westhoek et al., 2012). Crop rotations improve biodiversity and soil organic matter notably where fallow or legume crops are introduced into the rotation (Hart et al., 2016). Thus, benefits of introducing multiple crops in the farming system are related to their introduction in rotations, rather than in a diversification scheme.

The maintaining of permanent grassland as a means to reduce or avoid GHGs is not well targeted because current agricultural GHGs are mainly related to livestock farming activities and not so much to changes in land use (Pelikan et al., 2015). The regulation allows permanent grassland to be ploughed and reseeded as long as the land remains under grass. However, climate mitigation benefits through carbon sequestration would result only if the land maintained as permanent grassland is not ploughed or reseeded. Furthermore, the requirement to maintain permanent grassland is subject to *ex post* control. It is only when more than 5% of permanent grassland has been changed to other uses that the excess must be reverted to permanent grassland. At that stage, the detrimental effects on the environment would already have occurred (Söderberg, 2016).

In terms of changes in land use, a change in crop areas is observed. Areas under maize and durum wheat decrease. Nitrogen-fixing crop surfaces (mainly soya and alfalfa) increase, as 27 member states have chosen this option (Solazzo and Pierangeli, 2015; Solazzo et al., 2015). In Austria, the share of cover crops at national level declines by 48 percentage points. This is the result of the decrease in payments for sowing winter cover crops that leads to an increase in standard and reduced tillage (Kirchner et al., 2015). In Poland, the share of cereals falls by 0.4 percentage point (Was et al., 2014). It is also important to highlight that maintaining 95% of permanent grassland would provide sufficient reserve land to allow for a change in land use from grassland to crop land to respond to increasing global demand for food (Westhoek et al., 2012).

Greening measures could also lead to global trade impacts and global price changes as a result of the impacts on land use from the changes in farm practices. According to Pelikan et al. (2015) and based on the CAPRI and GTAP economic simulation models, greening may lead to a reduction of the supply of agricultural crops and higher crop prices in the European Union. The EFA requirement could lead to a 3.1%, decrease of oilseed production and boost prices by 2.7%. A study estimating changes in the cropping structure and economic results of Polish farms shows that the supply of agricultural products would be reduced as a result of the additional compliance costs of the greening requirements; leading to an increase in prices (Was et al., 2014). More studies conclude that greening measures, and particularly EFAs, reduce production and raise prices in the European Union (Cantore et al., 2011; Matthews, 2011).

---

80 – 4. ENVIRONMENTAL COMPONENTS

More specifically, the CAP 2014-20 scenario estimates an increase in total utilised agricultural area by 0.1%, while without greening that area would be reduced by 0.4%. Within the overall agricultural land area, some reallocations across crops occur. For example, the CAP 2014-20 scenario points to a decrease of 2% of the area under cereals and increases by 7% of the area under arable crops and by nearly 6% of the area set-aside and fallow. Results show that the aggregate effect of greening is likely to be small, however effects on some specific land allocations are notable. Under the "no-greening" scenario, utilised agricultural area is reduced by 0.4% and the area of cereals decreases by 0.4%, while other arable crops would increase by more than 8% and set-aside and fallow would decrease by 3%. *Animal numbers* (herd sizes) would increase in the no-greening scenario, though by less than 1%.

In most cases the results indicate that greening effects on production are less than 1%. Notable exceptions are increases in other arable crops and sheep and goats with 2.8% and 6% respectively in the no-greening scenario. As the impact on prices is concerned, supply effects on prices are observed and prices would be mostly down under the no-greening scenario both for crops and livestock products. However as for the production changes, the estimated prices changes are less than 1%. Similarly the impacts on *trade* (exports and imports) are small.

Table 4.3. CAP 2014-20 scenario and the no-greening scenario results

Relative differences to the baseline in the two scenarios

| Activity | Hectares Herd sizes | | Production | | Producer Prices | | Trade | | | |
| | | | | | | | Import | | Export | |
Scenario	CAP 2014-20	No Greening	CAP 2014-20	No Greening	CAP 2014-20	No Greening	CAP 2014-20	No Greening	CAP 2014-20	No Greening
Utilized agricultural area	0.1%	-0.4%	na	na	na	na	na	na	na	na
Cereals	-2.0%	-0.4%	-1.4%	-0.1%	1.8%	0.6%	0.4%	0.9%	-2.1%	-0.2%
Oilseeds	-0.4%	0.6%	-0.4%	0.3%	1.4%	0.5%	-1.0%	-1.3%	-2.9%	-1.2%
Other arable crops	7.4%	8.2%	1.7%	2.8%	-1.0%	-2.3%	-0.6%	-0.9%	1.4%	1.0%
- of which pulses	27.3%	28.8%	na	na	na	na	na	na	na	na
Vegetables and Permanent crops	0.0%	0.0%	0.0%	0.0%	0.2%	-0.1%	0.0%	0.0%	-0.1%	0.1%
Fodder activities	0.6%	-1.0%	na	na	na	na	na	na	na	na
Set aside and fallow land	5.7%	-3.0%	na	na	na	na	na	na	na	na
All ruminants	0.7%	0.7%	na	na	na	na	na	na	na	na
Meat	na	na	0.0%	0.1%	0.0%	-0.3%	0.1%	0.0%	0.0%	0.2%
All cattle activities	0.0%	0.1%	na	na	na	na	na	na	na	na
Beef meat activities	-0.1%	0.0%	0.1%	0.2%	-0.1%	-0.3%	0.0%	-0.1%	0.2%	0.2%
- Pork meat	na	na	-0.1%	0.0%	0.1%	-0.1%	0.0%	0.0%	-0.2%	0.0%
- Sheep and goat meat	na	na	5.8%	5.9%	-6.4%	-6.5%	-1.2%	-1.2%	9.8%	10.0%
- Poultry meat	na	na	-0.4%	-0.3%	0.3%	0.1%	0.5%	0.2%	-0.4%	-0.3%
Other Animal products	na	na	0.0%	0.1%	-0.1%	-0.3%	0.6%	0.4%	0.7%	0.7%
All Dairy	0.1%	0.1%	na	na	na	na	na	na	na	na
- Raw milk	na	na	0.0%	0.1%	-0.1%	-0.3%	0.0%	0.0%	0.1%	0.1%
- Eggs	na	na	-0.3%	-0.1%	0.5%	0.2%	0.6%	0.3%	-0.3%	-0.2%
Other animals	0.8%	0.9%	na	na	na	na	na	na	na	na
Pasture	1.9%	-1.3%	na	na	na	na	na	na	na	na
Arable land	-0.8%	0.0%	na	na	na	na	na	na	na	na

Source: CAPRI model results, 2016.

The CAPRI model also computes the amount of nitrogen that is added to the soil via fertilisation, crop residues, nitrogen fixation and atmospheric deposition, and subtracts the amount removed in the form of harvested crop products. The difference is a generally positive "N surplus". In reality, the link between nitrogen surplus and environmental impact depends on local soil, hydrological and climatic conditions as well as on technological details such as timing in application. That amount of detail cannot be modelled in CAPRI. Therefore, although limited in scope, N surplus is used as an indicator of environmental impact. All other things being equal, one can assume that a higher N surplus would increase nitrogen run-off and leaching.

Table 4.4 shows the nitrogen surplus both in gross terms "in sum", and divided by the total agricultural land area "per ha". The results do not lead to any decisive conclusion about the impacts of the CAP 2014-20 on nitrogen surplus. Total nitrogen surplus increases in some regions but decreases in others. The net effect on the entire European Union is close to zero.

Table 4.4. Nitrogen surplus at soil level, per country

	Reference		CAP after 2013		No-VCS		No-greening		Full flat rate	
	1000t/year	kg/ha	1000t/year	kg/ha	1000t/year	kg/ha	1000t/year	kg/ha	1000t/year	kg/ha
European Union 28	11 703	64	0.10%	0.00%	-0.30%	-0.40%	0.00%	0.80%	0.10%	-0.30%
Belgium	280	188	-0.30%	0.00%	-0.60%	-0.60%	0.00%	1.80%	-0.30%	-1.10%
Denmark	372	134	-0.70%	-0.80%	-0.80%	-0.10%	-0.40%	0.90%	-0.70%	-0.80%
Germany	1 080	62	0.20%	0.10%	0.20%	0.00%	0.10%	0.10%	0.20%	-0.20%
Austria	140	45	-0.40%	-0.30%	-0.40%	-0.10%	-0.90%	0.00%	-0.40%	0.10%
Netherlands	499	265	-0.40%	-0.20%	-0.40%	0.00%	-0.20%	0.30%	-0.40%	-0.30%
France	1 892	66	0.40%	-0.10%	-0.40%	-0.70%	0.00%	1.40%	0.40%	-0.60%
Portugal	153	44	-0.20%	-0.10%	-1.90%	-1.80%	-0.40%	1.60%	-0.20%	0.40%
Spain	1 182	51	0.20%	-0.10%	-0.50%	-0.60%	-0.50%	0.30%	0.00%	0.50%
Greece	218	43	-1.30%	0.80%	-2.00%	-1.10%	-2.30%	0.40%	-1.30%	0.50%
Italy	932	66	-0.50%	-0.50%	-0.90%	-0.40%	0.40%	1.70%	-0.50%	-1.20%
Ireland	487	116	-0.10%	0.00%	0.10%	0.20%	0.20%	0.20%	-0.10%	-0.40%
Finland	125	55	-0.70%	1.20%	-1.80%	-2.80%	-1.30%	2.60%	-0.70%	0.30%
Sweden	181	61	-1.10%	0.40%	-2.00%	-1.80%	-1.90%	1.50%	-1.10%	0.30%
United Kingdom	1 293	79	-0.10%	-0.10%	0.10%	0.20%	-0.10%	0.00%	-0.10%	-0.20%
Czech Republic	272	67	-1.40%	-1.10%	-1.50%	-0.30%	0.30%	2.10%	-1.30%	-1.70%
Estonia	59	62	2.80%	0.20%	2.10%	-0.60%	0.90%	1.20%	2.80%	-0.60%
Hungary	193	33	-0.70%	-0.70%	-1.10%	-0.50%	0.60%	2.50%	-0.70%	-1.90%
Lithuania	174	59	3.10%	0.60%	2.50%	0.10%	1.20%	0.40%	3.10%	-0.50%
Latvia	72	37	3.30%	0.10%	2.80%	0.10%	1.00%	0.60%	3.30%	-0.70%
Poland	1 183	70	1.00%	1.00%	0.50%	-0.60%	0.50%	0.40%	1.00%	0.20%
Slovenia	25	49	-0.80%	-0.90%	-2.00%	-1.10%	-0.90%	1.10%	-0.80%	0.10%
Slovak Republic	95	45	0.40%	0.50%	-0.30%	-0.70%	0.90%	1.30%	0.40%	-0.50%
Croatia	84	56	2.30%	1.20%	0.80%	-1.40%	0.90%	1.00%	2.30%	0.50%
Cyprus	16	97	0.00%	-1.40%	-0.20%	0.00%	-0.40%	1.10%	0.00%	-1.00%
Malta	3	270	-0.90%	2.70%	-0.30%	-2.70%	-0.90%	3.00%	-0.90%	-0.20%
Bulgaria	202	37	0.30%	0.20%	-1.20%	-1.50%	0.20%	2.40%	0.30%	-0.80%
Romania	491	34	-0.10%	0.20%	0.00%	0.00%	0.00%	0.00%	-0.10%	-0.10%

Source: CAPRI model results, 2016.

In the CAPRI model, despite the pillar 1 budget being spent on decoupled payments, the model considers these payments as not entirely decoupled because they keep land in production that could otherwise be made available for other uses. Only the "no-VCS" simulation leads to a reduction in total nitrogen-surplus at the EU level. However, this total reduction only amounts to 0.3 percentage points compared with the reference, which is not very significant.

The effects of decoupled area payments are also analysed in recent OECD work. Modelling results show that decoupled area payments increase production and negatively impact biodiversity and water quality (OECD, 2016b). Another report where the effects of stylised policies on productivity, climate change adaptation and mitigation in Finland are analysed finds that commodity production increases when decoupled payments are introduced, compared to a situation without agricultural or environmental support, as the profitability of keeping land that would have been left idle in agricultural use increases. In the absence of appropriate farming practices, the increase in production goes together with the increase of GHG emissions and nutrient runoff. The environmentally adjusted multifactor productivity and social welfare are lower than under the market solution, in the context depicted by this modelling work (OECD, 2016c).

The results on surpluses per hectare (in the table "kg/ha", measured in kg of N per hectare) contain the joint effect of changing production mix, land use and fertiliser application. This relative indicator adds some information to the environmental effects of CAP 2014-20. In terms of surpluses per hectare, the CAP 2014-20 package has ambiguous overall effects on N surpluses with some countries experiencing a decrease in N surplus, others an increase and yet others no change. However, if broken down into components, the voluntary coupled support generally increases N surplus per hectare, whereas the introduction of greening generally seems to reduce N surpluses. Among the factors generating the deterioration of N surplus under the VCS scenario are more mineral fertilizer, more manure and N from biofixation (due to support to pulses). However, the nutrients contained in the harvested crops, and thus N retention, concurrently increase depending on yields and crop mix. Finally, when scanning the results by countries, a full flat rate application of the basic payment appears to be somewhat more favourable from a nitrogen pressure point of view than the heterogeneous convergence model currently in place. Yet, the gross effects for EU28 point in the opposite direction and variability by country is large.

Although the results at EU level indicate that the policies analysed here have little impact on N surpluses, it cannot be excluded that there are larger impacts at a local scale, including eutrophication and pollution of drinking water resulting from N leaching at regional or local scale.

Overall assessment of the environmental components of the CAP 2014-20

The environmental components of the CAP should be considered as a whole and the greening payment should be evaluated together with other conditions, be they compulsory, i.e. cross-compliance, or voluntary, such as those associated with agri-environmental measures. This is important as it may influence member states' decisions with regards to budgetary transfers between pillars. Typically, pillar 1 measures are subject to compulsory environmental conditions and pillar 2 measures, with the exception of compensatory payments for compliance with Natura 2000 and the Water Framework Directive, are voluntary.

In essence, the greening direct payment applies uniform conditions on farming practices all over the European Union and offers a blanket support to all farms, thus it has the advantage of common and broad coverage. Although in practice some flexibility has been introduced in the implementation, it is ill adapted to the diversity of farming practices and conditions of the European Union. Furthermore only in a few cases can member states impose more stringent conditions.

Overall, the greening payment and associated conditions would positively impact the environment through land use change, while the effects are likely to be limited. This may be explained by the existing farming practices associated with the cross-compliance conditions that have applied to direct payments since 2005. As a result, compared to existing cross-compliance, the conditions attached to the greening payment would drive change in few additional areas. This is both because they do not expand the areas of agricultural land under environmental condition and also because the conditions imposed are not substantially different from the farming practices already implemented by farmers.

Most studies suggest that the effect of greening will depend largely on specific implementation conditions in member states and their regions. Moreover the type of impact will depend mostly on features at farm level and the environmental impact can be either positive or negative. Options are available that may enhance the beneficial impacts of greening on biodiversity and soil organic substance, such as combining crop diversification with crop rotation. However, they have not been adopted by member states. Such measures would be more constraining as they require monitoring over several years, whereas the implementation of the greening payment is annual. Meanwhile, the EFA has been identified as holding the potential to induce the greatest change (Söderberg, 2016). Yet, for this to happen, member states should be encouraged to promote the EFA features that offer the greatest environmental benefits.

The possibility given to member states to devolve the implementation of the CAP second pillar to regions could potentially improve the targeting and local relevance of its agri-environmental and investment measures in favour of better natural resource management and adaptation to climate change. As such they are likely to yield larger environmental benefits (Söderberg, 2016).

With regards to implementation conditions, analysis of cross-compliance had pointed to the fact that its positive environmental effects would be enhanced by facilitating compliance through simplification and improved farmer access to information and guidance (Söderberg, 2011). This also applies to greening. Farming practices must be adapted to the local environmental conditions in order to yield the expected environmental benefits. This highlights the important role of monitoring how and if farmers have indeed undertaken the greening requirements.

OECD (2016b) analysis has found that the environmental performance of the current policy mix is relatively good due to land area allocated to green set-aside and fertiliser application constraints in its agri-environmental scheme.

The current policy mix that combines production-oriented support, area-based support with support to the transition to environmentally friendly practices can be adapted to reinforce the capacity of agriculture to deliver beneficial environmental and climate change outcomes. Future CAP reforms should continue the long-term trend to increase the share of producer support with constraints on inputs. Recent work suggests that widening the policy mix to include crop insurance as a partial replacement for the BPS or the SAPS would improve environmentally adjusted productivity performance and social welfare (OECD, 2016b). First and foremost, an assessment of local conditions should be carried out in order to deliver support where it is needed.

Notes

1. Most of the relevant regulations apply across the farm sector and relate to the use of agricultural inputs, which have the potential to cause negative environmental effects. These regulatory requirements range from outright prohibitions, to input standards and resource-use requirements. In areas with higher environmental values (natural reserves), drinking water catchment areas, environmentally sensitive areas, stricter regulations may be applied. Over time, these regulatory requirements have become more stringent as awareness of environmental risk develops.

2. The detailed implementation and choices for crop diversification and rotation for each member state are not yet available.

3. In the United Kingdom (England, Northern Ireland and Wales) all grasslands within the Natura 2000 network have been designated as Environmentally Sensitive Permanent Grassland, while the ratio in the United Kingdom (Scotland) is 41%. As a result, the share is 62% for the United Kingdom.

References

Allen, B. and K. Hart (2013), "Meeting the EU's environmental challenges through the CAP - how do the reforms measure up?", in *Aspects of Applied Biology 118*: *Environmental Management on Farmland*, The Association of Applied Biologists IEEP, London.

Cantore, N., J. Kennan, S. Page (2011), "Cap reform and development: Introduction, reform options and suggestions for further research", Overseas Development institute, London, www.odi.org/sites/odi.org.uk/files/odi-assets/publications-opinion-files/7245.pdf.

EC (2016), Review of greening after one year, Commission staff working document, European Commission, Brussels, http://ec.europa.eu/agriculture/direct-support/pdf/2016-staff-working-document-greening-annex-4_en.pdf and http://ec.europa.eu/agriculture/direct-support/pdf/2016-staff-working-document-greening-annex-2_en.pdf (accessed February 2017).

EC (2011), Common Agricultural Policy towards 2020, Assessment of Alternative Policy Options, Commission Staff Working Paper, European Commission, http://ec.europa.eu/agriculture/policy-perspectives/impact-assessment/cap-towards-2020/report/full-text_en.pdf (accessed June 2016).

EC (2010), *Environmental impacts of different crop rotation in the EU*, Final report, European Commission, DG Environment, Brussels.

FOE Europe (2012), "Crop rotation: Benefiting farmers, the environment and the economy", Friends of Earth Europe, http://aprodev.eu/files/Trade/crop%20rotation%20briefing_pan_ifoam_aprodev_foee_fina.pdf (accessed August 2016).

Hart, K., (2015), "Green direct payments: implementation choices of 9 MS and their environmental implications", Institute for European Environmental Policy, London.

Hart, K. and G. Radley (2016), "Scoping the environmental implications of aspects of Pillar 1 reform 2014-2020", a report for the Land Use Policy Group, Institute for European Environmental Policy, London, www.snh.gov.uk/docs/A1897544.pdf (accessed in June 2016).

Hart, K., K. Buckwell and D. Baldock (2016), "Learning the lessons of the Greening of the CAP", a report for the UK Land Use Policy Group in collaboration with the European Nature Conservation Agencies Network, Institute for European Environmental Policy, London.

Kirchner, M., M. Schönhart and E. Schmid (2015), "The impacts of CAP post-2013 and regional climate change on agricultural land use intensity and the environment in Austria", International Association of Agricultural Economists, 29th International Conference of Agricultural Economists, University of Natural Resources and Life Sciences Vienna, Austria, http://ageconsearch.umn.edu/bitstream/212004/2/Kirchner-The%20impacts%20of%20CAP%20post-2013%20and%20regional%20climate%20change-839.pdf (accessed June 2016).

Mahy, L., et al. (2014), "Simulating farm level response to crop diversification policy", Department of Agricultural Economics, Ghent University, Belgium.

Mathews, A. (2011), "Post-2013 EU Common Agricultural Policy, Trade and Development: A Review of Legislative Proposals", ICTSD Programme on Agricultural Trade and Sustainable Development, Issue Paper No.39, International Centre for Trade and Sustainable Development, Geneva, Switzerland.

Mili, S., L. Judez and R. De Andrés (2015), "Effects of New CAP Reform and Trends in Sustainable Olive Growing Systems in Southern Spain", International Association of Agricultural Economists, 2015 Conference, August 9-15, Milan, Italy, http://purl.umn.edu/212462 (accessed June 2016).

OECD (2016a), *Agricultural Policy Monitoring and Evaluation 2016*, OECD Publishing, Paris, http://dx.doi.org/10.1787/agr_pol-2016-en.

OECD (2016b), "Land use and ecosystem services in agriculture", forthcoming.

OECD (2016c), "Synergies and trade-offs between adaptation, mitigation and agricultural productivity: quantitative results of the model application with data from Finland"; forthcoming.

OECD (2015), *OECD Review of Agricultural Policies: Switzerland 2015*, OECD Publishing, Paris, http://dx.doi.org/10.1787/9789264168039-en.

OECD/FAO (2016), *OECD-FAO Agricultural Outlook 2016-2025*, OECD Publishing, Paris, http://dx.doi.org/10.1787/agr_outlook-2016-en.

Pelikan, J., W. Britz and T. W. Hertel (2015), "Green Light for Green Agricultural Policies? An analysis at Regional and Global Scales", *Journal of Agricultural Economics*, Vol. 66, No. 1, http://onlinelibrary.wiley.com/doi/10.1111/1477-9552.12065/full (accessed June 2016).

Rousset, S. et al. (2015), "Voluntary environmental and organic standards in agriculture: Policy implications", *OECD Food, Agriculture and Fisheries Papers*, No. 86, OECD Publishing, Paris. http://dx.doi.org/10.1787/5jrw8fg0rr8x-en.

Söderberg, T. (ed.) (2016), *Greening of the CAP in practice – costs versus environmental benefits*, Report 2016:18Eng, Swedish Board of Agriculture, Jönköping.

Söderberg, T. (ed.) (2011), "Environmental Effects of Cross-Compliance", Report 2011:5Eng, Swedish Board of Agriculture, Jönköping.

Solazzo, R. and F. Pierangeli (2015), "A two-step modelling approach for the impact assessment of greening in Italy", Consiglio per la ricerca in agricoltura e l'analisi dell'economia agrarian, http://ageconsearch.umn.edu/bitstream/212246/2/Solazzo.pdf (accessed June 2016).

Solazzo, R., M. Donati and F. Arfini (2015), "Impact assessment of greening and the issue of nitrogen-fixing crops – Evidence from northern Italy", Outlook on Agriculture, Vol. 44, pp.215-222, https://doi.org/10.5367/oa.2015.0215.

Was, A., E. Majewski and S. Czekaj (2014), "Impacts of CAP 'Greening' on Polish Farms", paper prepared for presentation at the EAAE 2014 Congress, August 26 to 29, Ljubljana, Slovenia, http://ageconsearch.umn.edu/bitstream/182699/2/W%C4%85s-Impacts_of_CAP_%E2%80%9Cgreening%E2%80%9D_on_Polish_farms-608_a.pdf (accessed June 2016).

Westhoek, H. et al. (2012), "Greening the CAP, An analysis of the effects of the European Commission's proposals for the Common Agricultural Policy 2014-2020", PBL Note, PBL publication number 500136007, PBL Netherlands Environmental Assessment Agency, The Hague.

Annex 4.A1.

Decentralised implementation of the pillar 2 agri-environment and climate measures in the Centre-Val de Loire region of France

General features of Centre-Val de Loire region

The Centre-Val de Loire region is located in the French central plateau benefitting from a temperate oceanic climate. Agriculture is an important sector in the region as it is the first regional producer of wheat and oilseed in the European Union and it contributes 73% of France's sugar beet production. The region is also an important producer of other cereals, horticultural products, wine and a large variety of livestock products. The region has allocated 23% of its RDP funds to AECM, above the EU28 average of 19% (Table 4.A1.1).

Table 4.A1.1. Contextual information on Centre-Val de Loire region (France)

Population		2.5 million	
Total land area		4 million ha	
Share of rural area		67%	
Share of utilised agricultural area		60%	
Average farm holding area		100 ha	
Main crops	Share of utilised agricultural area		Production (tonnes)
Soft wheat	25%		5 000 000
Durum wheat	3%		450 000
Maize	7%		1 683 300
Rapeseed	12%		1 080 000
Other oilseeds	16%		190 000
Protein crops	11%		98 000
Sugar beet	13%		2 825 000
Total RDP budget		EUR 530 million	
Total budget for AECM	EUR 124 million		23% of RDP budget
EAFRD contribution	EUR 80 million		65% of AECM budget
National co-funding	EUR 26 million		21% of AECM budget
Additional national and local funding	EUR 18 million		15% or AECM budget

Notes: RDP = Rural Development Programme; EAFRD = European Agricultural Fund for Rural Development; AECM = Agri-environment and climate measure; Shares of AECM budget do not add up to 100 because of rounding.

Sources: Eurostat, European Commission and OECD calculations based on national 2014-20 RDP budget as published in: http://ec.europa.eu/agriculture/rural-development-2014-2020/country-files/index_en.htm, 2016.

Along with the decentralised implementation mode, the regional council in Centre-Val de Loire carried out a regional diagnosis of the territory to define its regional RDP. This diagnostic highlighted the following regional issues: increasing number of cities within nitrate-vulnerable areas, decreasing quality of water (due to leaching nitrates and pesticides) and an erosion of biodiversity in agricultural land. Following this diagnosis, the regional council has focused its AECMs on water and biodiversity. The regional council then identified areas with local specificities related to these two issues, which led to a mapping of zones for priority action (ZAP in French). The ZAPs in Centre-Val de Loire are based on both issues of biodiversity (comprising 50% of the regional territory) and water (100% of the regional territory). According to the regional RDP, the AECMs selected contribute to adapting local agriculture to climate change through support of pastures preservation, forage autonomy, carbon sequestration and reduction of mineral fertilisation. Overall, Centre-Val de Loire has enrolled 171 000 ha of land under AECM, representing 7.4% of its total agricultural area.

A local example of AECM targeting crop-livestock farming systems

The local administrative unit called "Cher" within the Centre-Val de Loire region harbours a specific AECM promoting a mixed crop and ruminant farming system to increase local feed self-sufficiency. The local territory mapped for this AECM comprises 185 administrative communes, representing 260 000 ha, where ruminant farms are dominant. The targeted AECM thus aims to introduce more grass into the crop rotation (in particular, with spring rotational grazing), to diversify the number of forage crops to reduce the share of maize in the area allotted to forage crops, and to decrease the use of manufactured concentrate feed. An expected outcome of the new farming system where activity is split more evenly between livestock and crops is to allow farmers to hedge their agricultural risk with both activities.

All the agricultural land of eligible holdings can be enrolled in the measure except land under perennial crops. To be eligible, farmers have to fulfil several conditions (Table 4.A1.2). Every hectare enrolled will receive EUR 263.51 per year during for 5 years. The yearly payment ceiling for this AECM is set at EUR 20 000 per holding. The measure is funded for 75% by the European Agricultural Fund for Rural Development and for 25% by the French Ministry of Agriculture, Food and Forestry.

Table 4.A1.2. Enrolment and project specifications for the mixed crop and ruminant farming system agri-environment and climate measure in the Cher

At enrolment	More than half of the utilised agricultural area (UAA) is within the territory where the project is implemented Share of grass in the UAA is below 80% Share of staple crops in the UAA is below 53%
Throughout the five years	Maintain the livestock sector activity and detain more than 10 ruminant livestock units (LSU) No ploughing of permanent pastures Ban on using animal growth regulators except barley malt Make use of technical support on nitrogen management
From year 3	Share of grass area is at least 47% of UAA Maintain up to 25% of area for forage crops under maize Respect annual ceiling level for purchases of manufactured feed[1] Achieve 25% reduction target for treatment frequency index (TFI) of herbicides Achieve 35% reduction target for TFI of insecticides and fungicides
Year 5	Achieve 40% reduction target for TFI of herbicides Achieve 50% reduction target for TFI of insecticides and fungicides

1. The maximum annual level for purchasing manufactured feed is 800 kg per bovine or equine LSU; 1 000 kg per ovine LSU; and 1 600 kg per goat LSU.

These decentralised AECMs at local and regional levels are framed and monitored to be consistent with the AECMs at national level. Thus, from the lowest geographical scale to the highest, the AECP described above is consistent with the regional rural development programme, which is itself consistent with the national RDP, which is itself consistent to the CAP's pillar 2. By decentralising its implementation of the RDP, the French government has delegated its authority to local relevant bodies. This contributes to respond better to local issues and to address implementation problems identified by the evaluation of the previous CAP RDP.

Sources to Annex 4.A1:

Eurostat database, Importance of rural areas, Regional table by NUTS and by Rural development programme, http://ec.europa.eu/agriculture/statistics/rural-development/2013/index_en.htm.

European Commission (2016), Rural Development 2014-2020 Country files website, http://ec.europa.eu/agriculture/rural-development-2014-2020/country-files/index_en.htm.

European Commission (2016), "Factsheet sur le programme de développement rural 2014-2020 de la région Centre Val-de-Loire", http://ec.europa.eu/agriculture/rural-development-2014-2020/country-files/fr/factsheet-centre-val-de-loire_fr.pdf.

European Parliament and Council (2013), Regulation (EU) No 1305/2013 of 17 December 2013 on support for rural development by the EAFRD and repealing Council Regulation (EC) No 1698/2005, http://eur-lex.europa.eu/legal-content/EN/TXT/?uri=celex:32013R1305.

Chambre d'Agriculture Cher (2016), "Notice spécifique de la mesure « MAEC système polyculture élevage herbivores dominante élevage, évolution de pratiques, niveau 2 » - « CE_18VL_SPE2 » du territoire Vallées de la Loire et de l'Allier", Campagne 2015, http://www.cher.chambagri.fr/uploads/media/CE_18VL_SPE2_160405_01.pdf.

Annex 4.A2.

Implementation of the greening conditions by member states

Member states	30% EU budget (EUR)	Implementation description
Austria	1 245 738	**Equivalent mechanism under an** agri-environment and climate measure: participation in the measure: more demanding crop diversification + EFA *"Environmentally sound and biodiversity-promoting types of management (UBB)" substitutes the requirements regarding EFA and crop diversification* **EFA** Eight types of EFA: land lying fallow, 4 landscape features, areas with short rotation coppice, areas with catch crops or green cover, areas with N-fixing crops + More demanding EFA: Creation of biodiversity protection sites on arable land (equivalent practice) **Permanent grassland** National level ESPG in Natura 2000[1]: 6% **Crop diversification** Equivalent practice "creation of biodiversity protection sites on arable land": minimum three-crop requirement, maximum of 75% for cereals and maize, maximum of 66% for the main crop
Belgium	903 483	**Permanent grassland** Regional level Total ESPG: 42% Flanders: 50% Wallonia: 35%
Belgium-FL		**EFA** Collective approach Fourteen types of EFA: land lying fallow, 5 landscape features, buffer strips, Ha of agro-forestry, strips of ha along forest edges with and without production, areas with short rotation coppice, afforested areas, areas with catch crops or green cover, areas with N-fixing crops
Belgium-WA		**EFA** Fourteen types of EFA: Land lying fallow, 7 landscape features, buffer strips, Ha of agro-forestry, strips of ha along forest edges without production, areas with short rotation coppice, areas with catch crops or green cover, areas with N-fixing crops
Bulgaria	1 408 280	**EFA** Fourteen types of EFA: land lying fallow, terraces, 7 landscapes features, buffer strips, strips of areas along forest edges without production, areas with short rotation coppice, areas with catch crops or green cover, areas with N-fixing crops **Permanent grassland** National level ESPG: 100%
Croatia	457 240	**EFA** Thirteen types of EFA: land lying fallow, 7 landscape features, buffer strips, strips of ha along forest edges without production, areas with short rotation coppice, areas with catch crops or green cover, areas with N-fixing crops **Permanent grassland** National level ESPG: 80%

Member states	30% EU budget (EUR)	Implementation description
Cyprus	89 134	**EFA** Five types of EFA: land lying fallow, buffer strips, ha of agro-forestry, afforested areas, N-fixing crops **Permanent grassland** National level ESPG: 72%
Czech Republic	1 538 493	**Equivalent mechanism under greening** through the agro-environment and climate measure **EFA** Eleven types of EFA: land lying fallow, terraces, 5 landscape features, areas with short rotation coppice, afforested areas, areas with catch crops or green cover, areas with N-fixing crops **Permanent grassland** National level ESPG: 100%
Denmark	1 525 241	**EFA** Six types of EFA: land lying fallow, 2 landscape features, buffer strips, areas with catch crops or green cover, areas with short rotation coppice **Permanent grassland** National level ESPG: 20%
Estonia	239 973	**EFA** Eighteen types: land lying fallow, 5 landscape features, areas with short rotation coppice, areas with N-fixing crops **Permanent grassland** National level ESPG: 1% **Crop diversification**
Finland	943 071	Regional application of green payments **EFA** Four types: land lying fallow, areas with short rotation coppice, areas with N-fixing crops **Permanent grassland** National level ESPG: 100%
France	13 095 854	**Equivalent mechanism** under certification scheme: suitable for single-crop maize farming to replace the crop diversification requirement with a **winter soil cover** **EFA** Eighteen types: land lying fallow, terraces, 8 landscape features, buffer strips, ha of agro-forestry, strips of ha along forest edges with and without production, areas with short rotation coppice, afforested areas, areas with catch crops or green cover, areas with N-fixing crops **Permanent grassland** Regional level ESPG: 63% **Crop diversification** The equivalence gives farmers the option to meet the greening requirements by sowing a winter green cover on land used for monoculture maize production (green cover replaces the requirement on diversification only for specialized producers of maize)
Germany	8 781 783	**EFA** 17 types: land lying fallow, terraces, 8 landscape features, buffer strips, ha of agro-forestry, strips of ha along forest edges without production, areas with short rotation coppice, afforested areas, areas with catch crops or green cover, areas with N-fixing crops **Permanent grassland** Regional level ESPG: 64%

Member states	30% EU budget (EUR)	Implementation description
Greece	3 395 616	**Regional application of green payments** **EFA** Six types: land lying fallow, 3 landscape features, buffer strips, areas with N-fixing crops **Permanent grassland** National level ESPG: 100%
Hungary	1 992 789	**EFA** Eighteen types: land lying fallow, terraces, 8 landscape features, buffer strips, ha of agro-forestry, strips of ha along forest edges with and without production, areas with short rotation coppice, afforested areas, areas with catch crops or green cover, areas with N-fixing crops **Permanent grassland** National level ESPG: 100%
Ireland	2 182 195	**Equivalent mechanism under an** agri-environment and climate measure **EFA** Eleven types: land lying fallow, 5 landscape features, buffer strips, areas with short rotation coppice, afforested areas, areas with catch crops or green cover, areas with N-fixing crops **Permanent grassland** National level ESPG: 2% **Crop diversification** Equivalent practice for crop diversification under AECM: sowing catch crop: winter cover on cropped areas
Italy	6 813 898	**Equivalent mechanism under greening** through the agro-environment and climate measure **EFA** Eighteen types: land lying fallow, terraces, 9 landscape features, buffer strips, ha of agro-forestry, areas of ha along forest edges with and without production, areas with short rotation coppice, afforested areas, areas with N-fixing crops **Permanent grassland** National level ESPG: 100%
Latvia	436 631	**EFA** Eight types: land lying fallow, 4 landscape features, buffer strips, areas with catch crops or green cover, areas with N-fixing crops **Permanent grassland** National level ESPG: 3%
Lithuania	856 072	**EFA** Two types: land lying fallow, areas with N-fixing crops **Permanent grassland** National level ESPG: 42%
Luxembourg	60 288	**EFA** Fifteen types: land lying fallow, 6 landscape features, buffer strips, ha of agro-forestry, strips of ha along forest edges with and without production, areas with short rotation coppice, afforested areas, areas with catch crops or green cover, areas with N-fixing crops **Permanent grassland** National level ESPG: 25%

Member states	30% EU budget (EUR)	Implementation description
Malta	9 270	**EFA** Seven types; land lying fallow, 5 landscape features, areas with N-fixing crops **Permanent grassland** No grassland
Netherlands	1 306 911	**Equivalent mechanism:** 3 certification schemes **EFA** Collective approach Four types: 1 landscape feature, areas with short rotation coppice, areas with catch crops or green cover, areas with N-fixing crops **Permanent grassland** National level ESPG: 100%
Poland	6 038 707	**Equivalent mechanism under an** agri-environment and climate measure **EFA** Collective approach Fifteen types: land lying fallow, 7 landscape features, buffer strips, strips of ha along forest edges with and without production, areas with short rotation coppice, afforested areas, areas with catch crops or green cover, areas with N-fixing crops **Permanent grassland** National level ESPG: 1% **Crop diversification** Equivalent practice: a minimum four-crop requirement, a 65% maximum for the main crop and all cereals, and a 10% minimum for all crops
Portugal	1 053 372	**EFA** Five types: Land lying fallow, 1 landscape feature, ha of agro-forestry, afforested areas, areas with N-fixing corps **Permanent grassland** National level ESPG: 1%
Romania	3 255 902	**EFA** 13 types: terraces, 7 landscape features, buffer strips, areas with short rotation coppice, afforested areas, areas with catch crops or green cover, areas with N-fixing crops **Permanent grassland** National level ESPG: /
Slovenia	244 405	**EFA** Three types: land lying fallow, areas with catch crops or green cover, areas with N-fixing crops **Permanent grassland** National level ESPG: 26%
Slovakia	785 583	**EFA** Ten types: land lying fallow, terraces, 4 landscape features, buffer strips, areas with short rotation coppice, areas with catch crops or green cover, areas with N-fixing crops **Permanent grassland** National level ESPG: 100%
Spain	7 315 578	**EFA** Four types: land lying fallow, ha of agro-forestry, afforested areas, areas with N-fixing crops **Permanent grassland** National level ESPG: 100%

Member states	30% EU budget (EUR)	Implementation description
Sweden	1 257 036	**EFA** Six types: land lying fallow, 1 landscape feature, areas with short rotation coppice, areas with catch crops or green cover, areas with N-fixing crops **Permanent grassland** National level ESPG: 100%
United Kingdom	5 859 669	**Permanent grassland** Regional level (EN, NI, SC, WA) Total UK ESPG: 62% England: 100% NI: 100% Scotland: 41% Wales: 100%
UK-England		**EFA** Six types: land lying fallow, 1 landscape feature, buffer strips, areas with catch crops or green cover, areas with N-fixing crops
UK-Northern Ireland		**EFA** Nine types: land lying fallow, 4 landscape features, ha of agro-forestry, areas with short rotation coppice, afforested areas, areas with N-fixing crops
UK-Scotland		**Sub-regional application** of green payment (Scotland's regions) **EFA** Five types: land lying fallow, 1 landscape feature, buffer strips, areas with catch crops or green cover, areas with N-fixing crops
UK-Wales		**EFA** Six types: land lying fallow, 2 landscape features, areas with short rotation coppice, afforested areas, areas with N-fixing crops

1. Share of grassland designated as Environmentally Sensitive Permanent Grassland by member states in Natura 2000 grassland.

Note by Turkey: The information in this document with reference to "Cyprus" relates to the southern part of the Island. There is no single authority representing both Turkish and Greek Cypriot people on the Island. Turkey recognises the Turkish Republic of Northern Cyprus (TRNC). Until a lasting and equitable solution is found within the context of the United Nations, Turkey shall preserve its position concerning the "Cyprus issue".

Note by all the European Union Member States of the OECD and the European Union: The Republic of Cyprus is recognised by all members of the United Nations with the exception of Turkey. The information in this document relates to the area under the effective control of the Government of the Republic of Cyprus.

Source: National Rural Development Programmes as published in Rural development 2014-2020: Country files. http://ec.europa.eu/agriculture/rural-development-2014-2020/country-files/, 2016.

ORGANISATION FOR ECONOMIC CO-OPERATION AND DEVELOPMENT

The OECD is a unique forum where governments work together to address the economic, social and environmental challenges of globalisation. The OECD is also at the forefront of efforts to understand and to help governments respond to new developments and concerns, such as corporate governance, the information economy and the challenges of an ageing population. The Organisation provides a setting where governments can compare policy experiences, seek answers to common problems, identify good practice and work to co-ordinate domestic and international policies.

The OECD member countries are: Australia, Austria, Belgium, Canada, Chile, the Czech Republic, Denmark, Estonia, Finland, France, Germany, Greece, Hungary, Iceland, Ireland, Israel, Italy, Japan, Korea, Latvia, Luxembourg, Mexico, the Netherlands, New Zealand, Norway, Poland, Portugal, the Slovak Republic, Slovenia, Spain, Sweden, Switzerland, Turkey, the United Kingdom and the United States. The European Union takes part in the work of the OECD.

OECD Publishing disseminates widely the results of the Organisation's statistics gathering and research on economic, social and environmental issues, as well as the conventions, guidelines and standards agreed by its members.

OECD PUBLISHING, 2, rue André-Pascal, 75775 PARIS CEDEX 16
(51 2017 09 1 P) ISBN 978-92-64-27868-4 – 2017